CURVILINEAR DESIGNS

A VICTORIAN SOURCEBOOK

GEORGE PHILLIPS

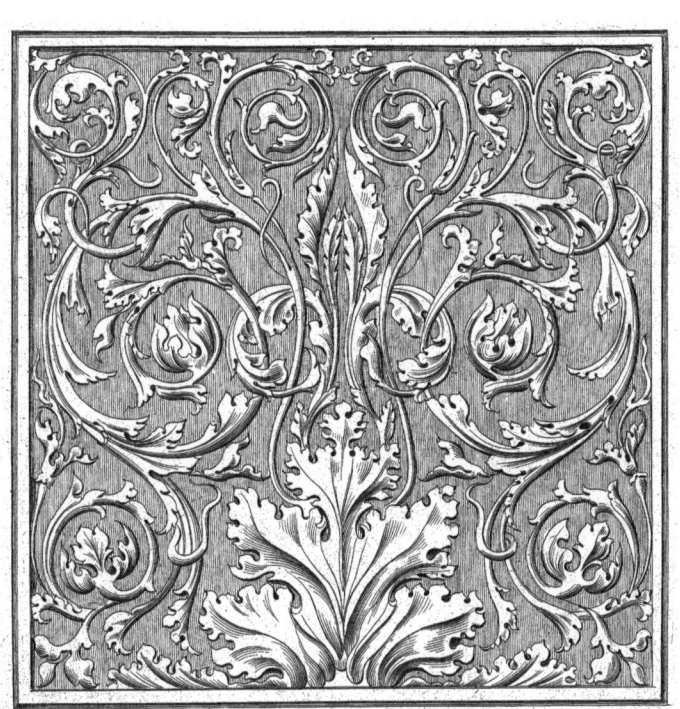

DOVER PUBLICATIONS, INC.
MINEOLA, NEW YORK

Bibliographical Note

This Dover edition, first published in 2012, contains all of the full-page plates from
Rudiments of Curvilinear Design, originally published by Shaw and Sons, London, in 1839.

International Standard Book Number
ISBN-13: 978-0-486-48976-6
ISBN-10: 0-486-48976-0

Manufactured in the United States by Courier Corporation
48976001
www.doverpublications.com

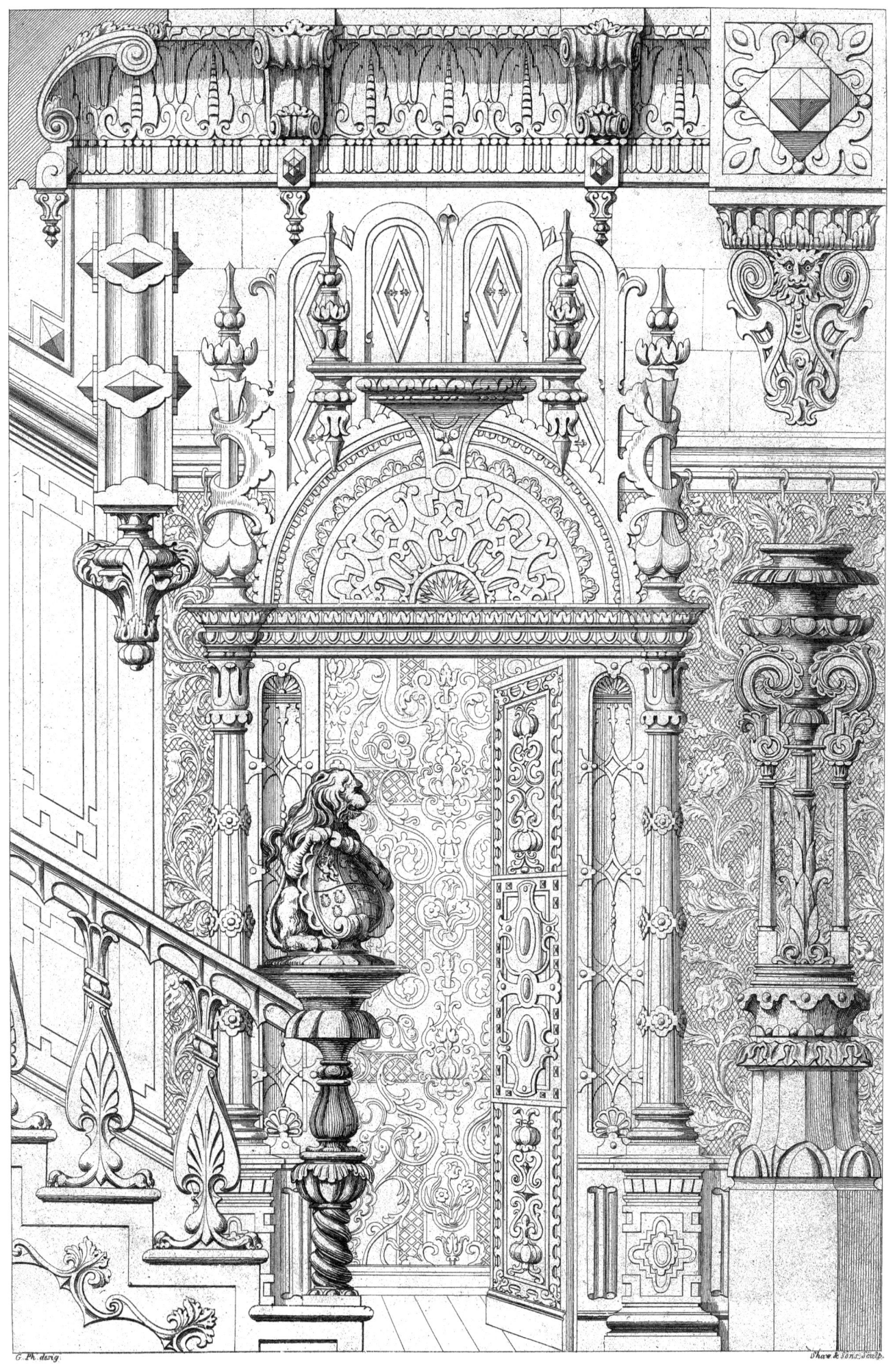

ELIZABETHAN

PLATE 1

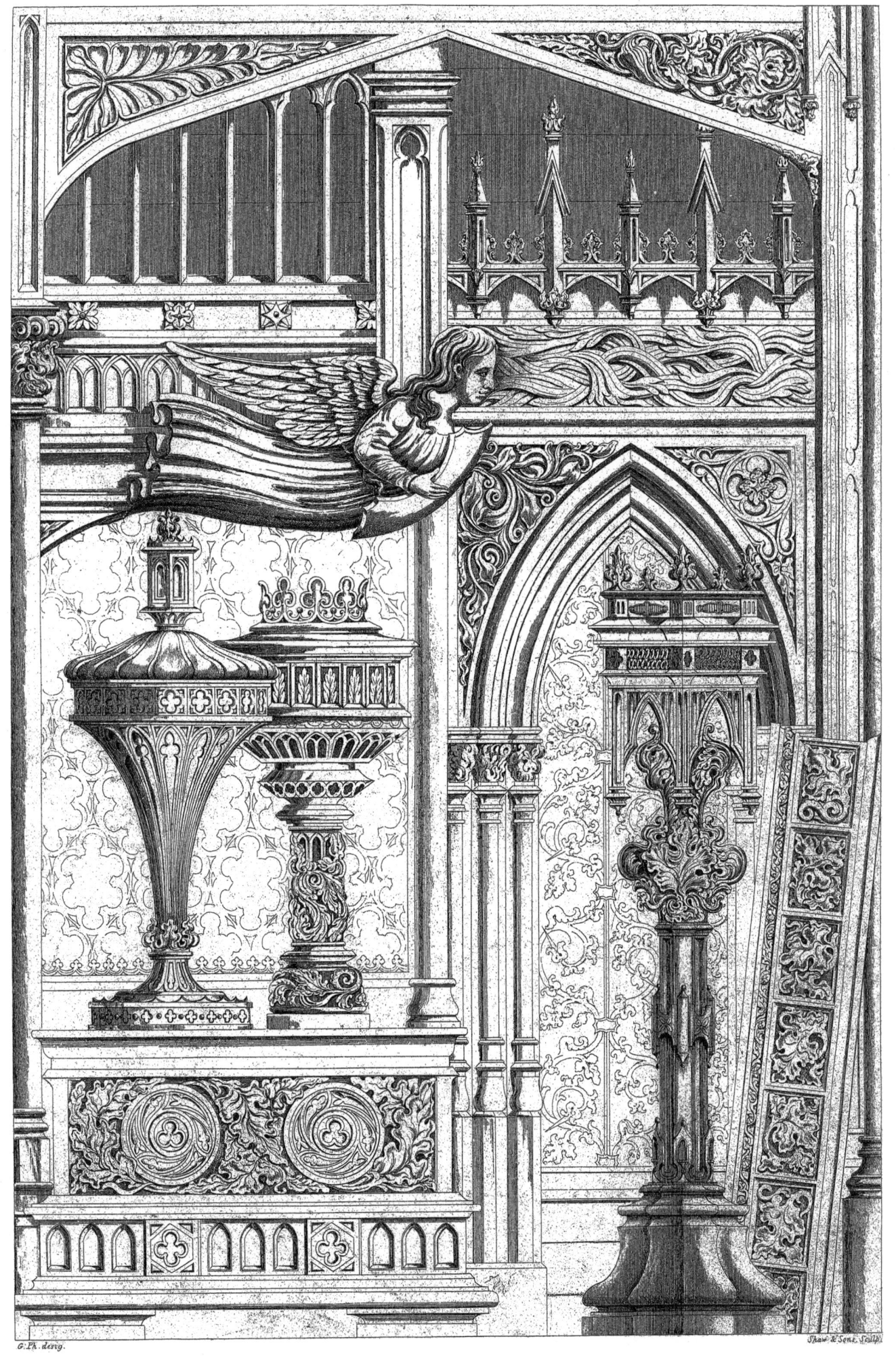

G.Ph. desig.

Shaw & Sons Sculp.

GOTHIC

PLATE 2

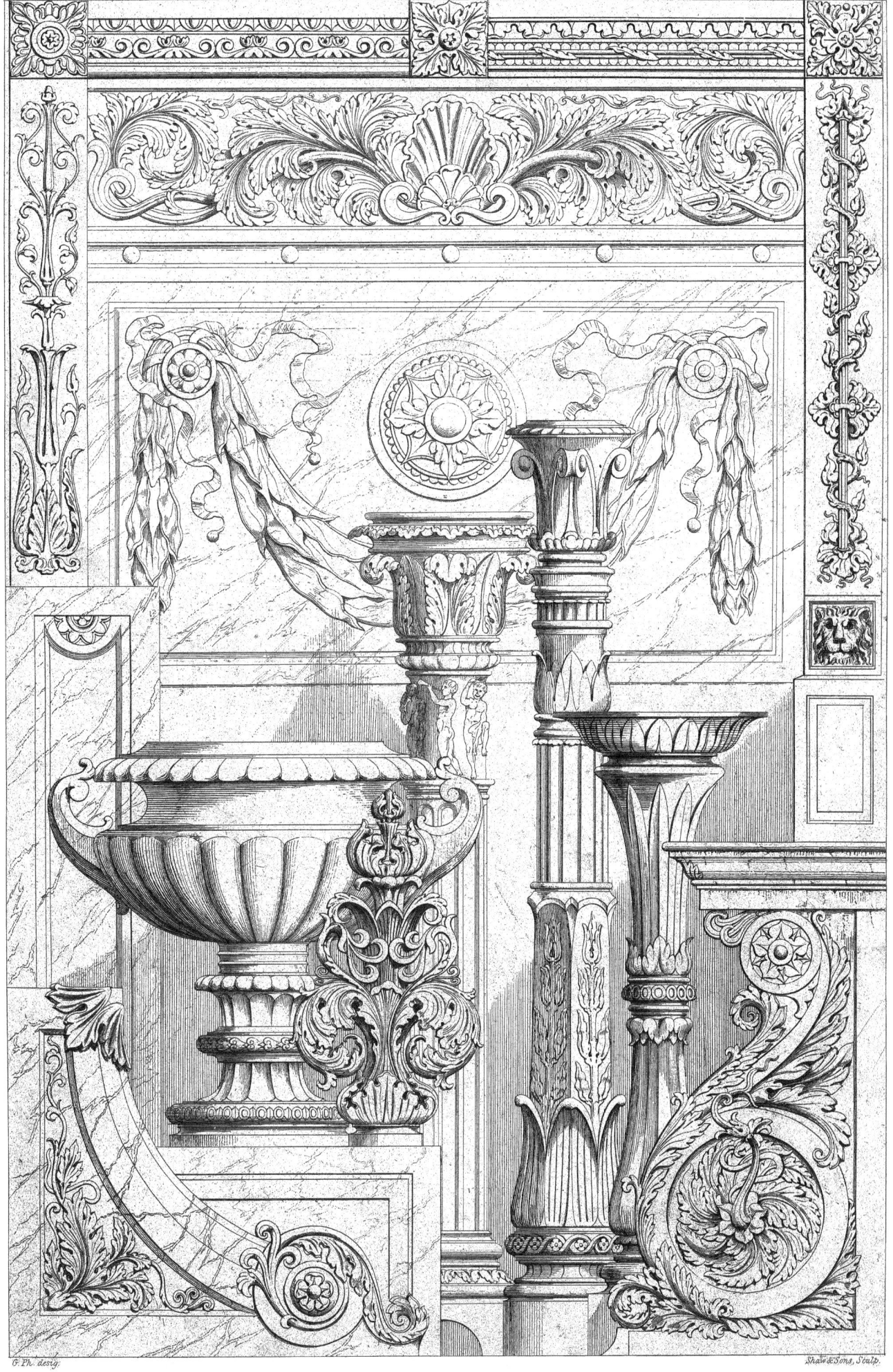

ROMAN

PLATE 3

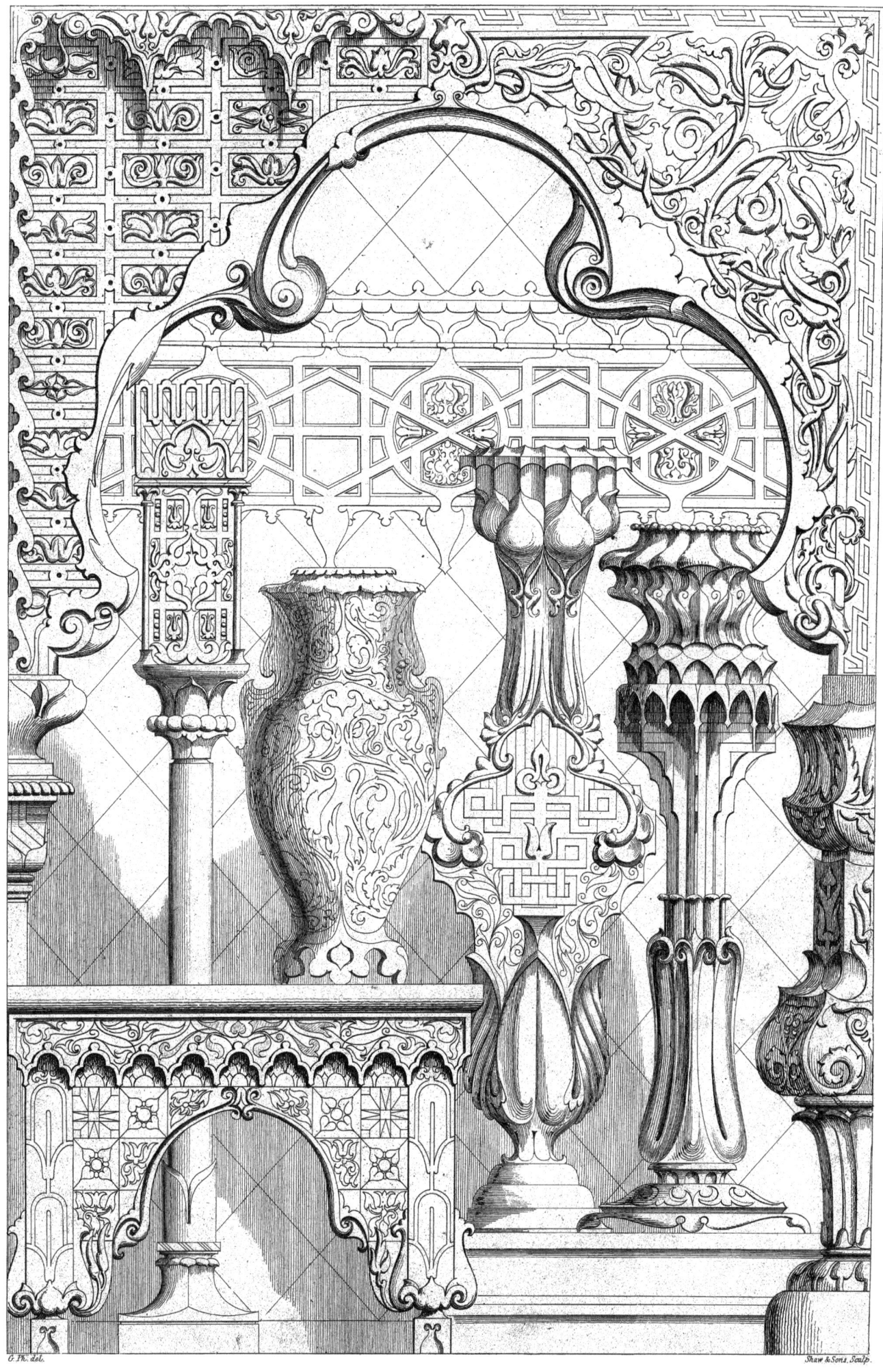

MORESQUE

PLATE 4

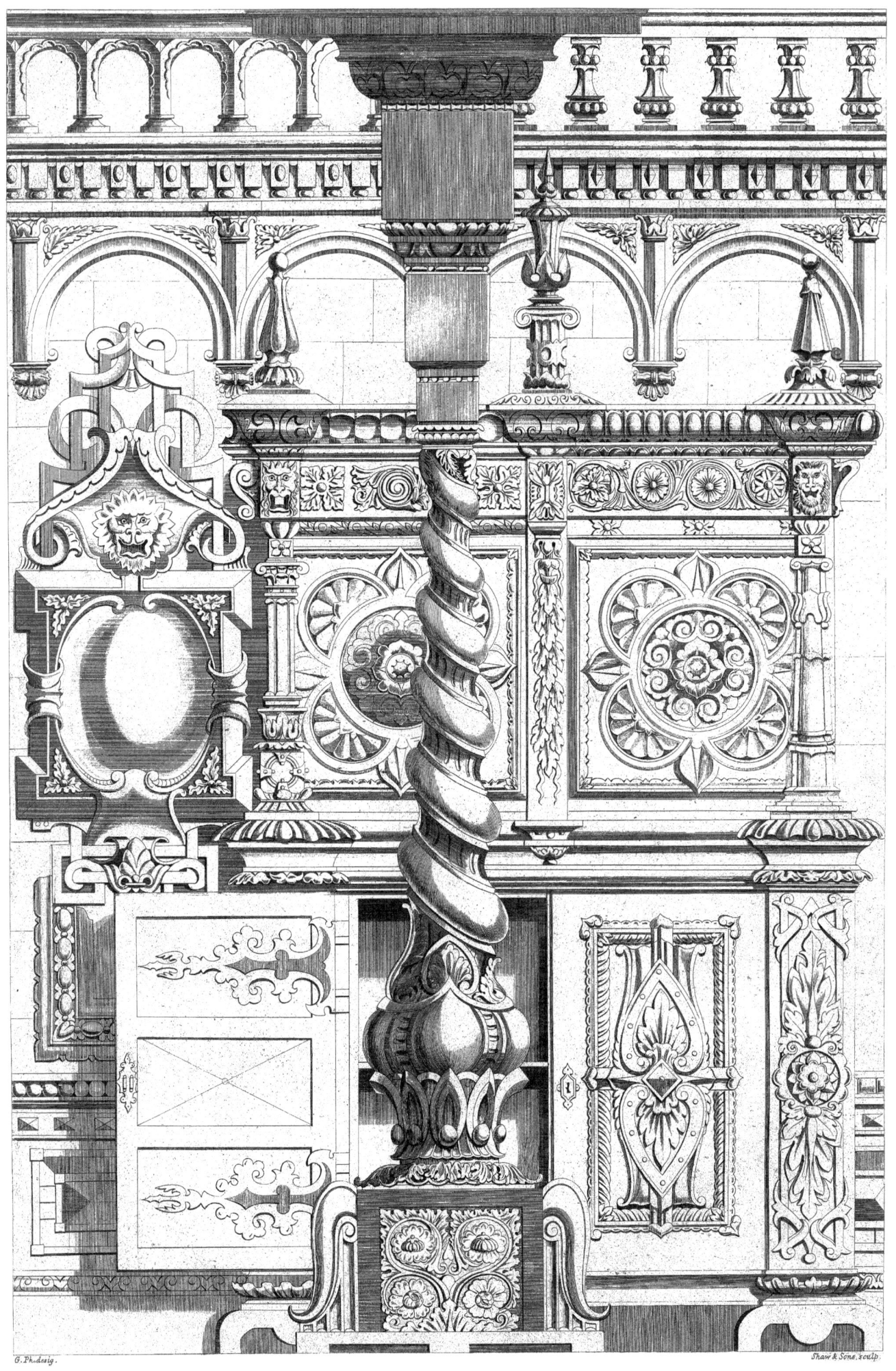

ELIZABETHAN

PLATE 5

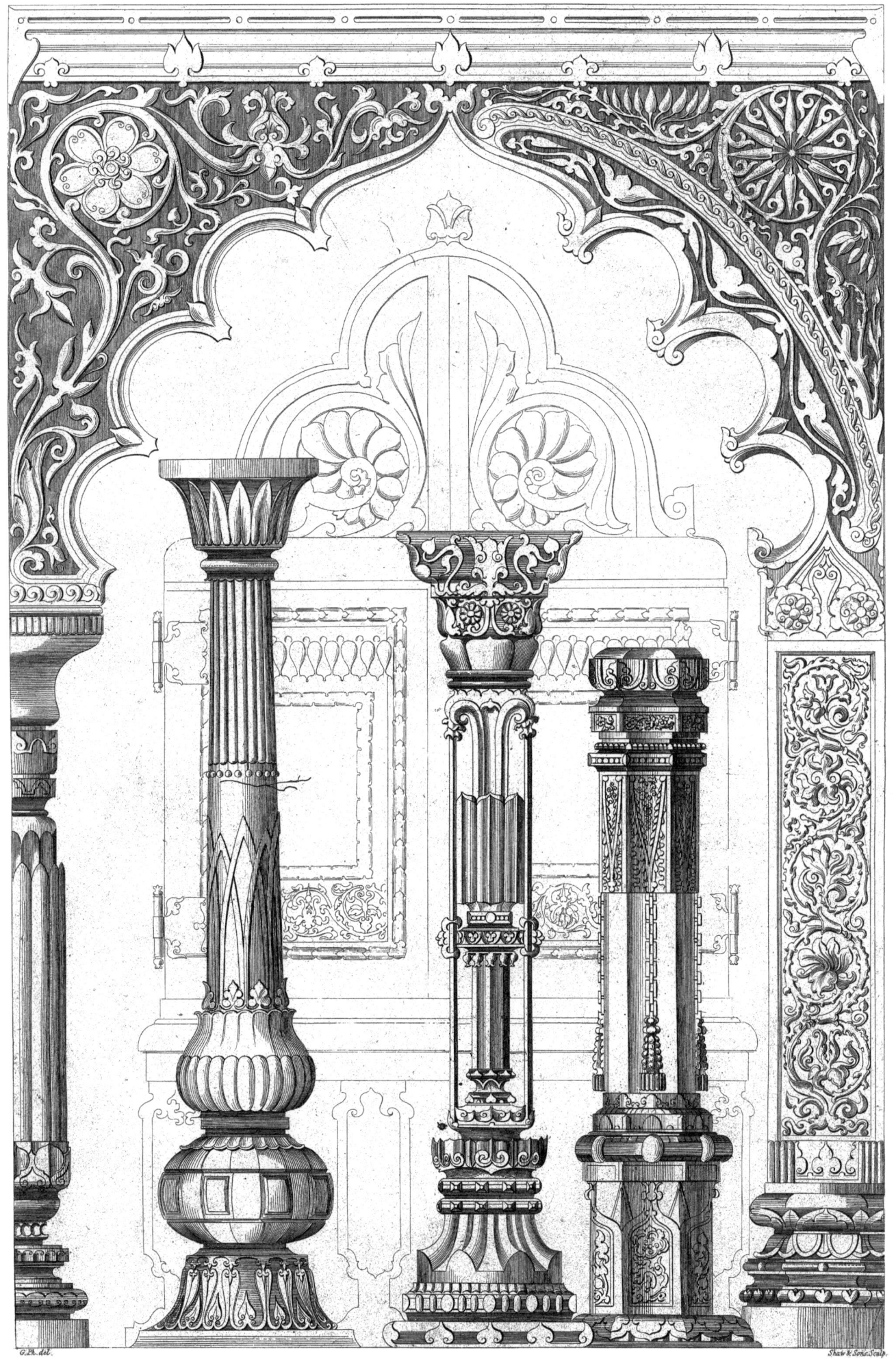

HINDOSTANEE

PLATE 6

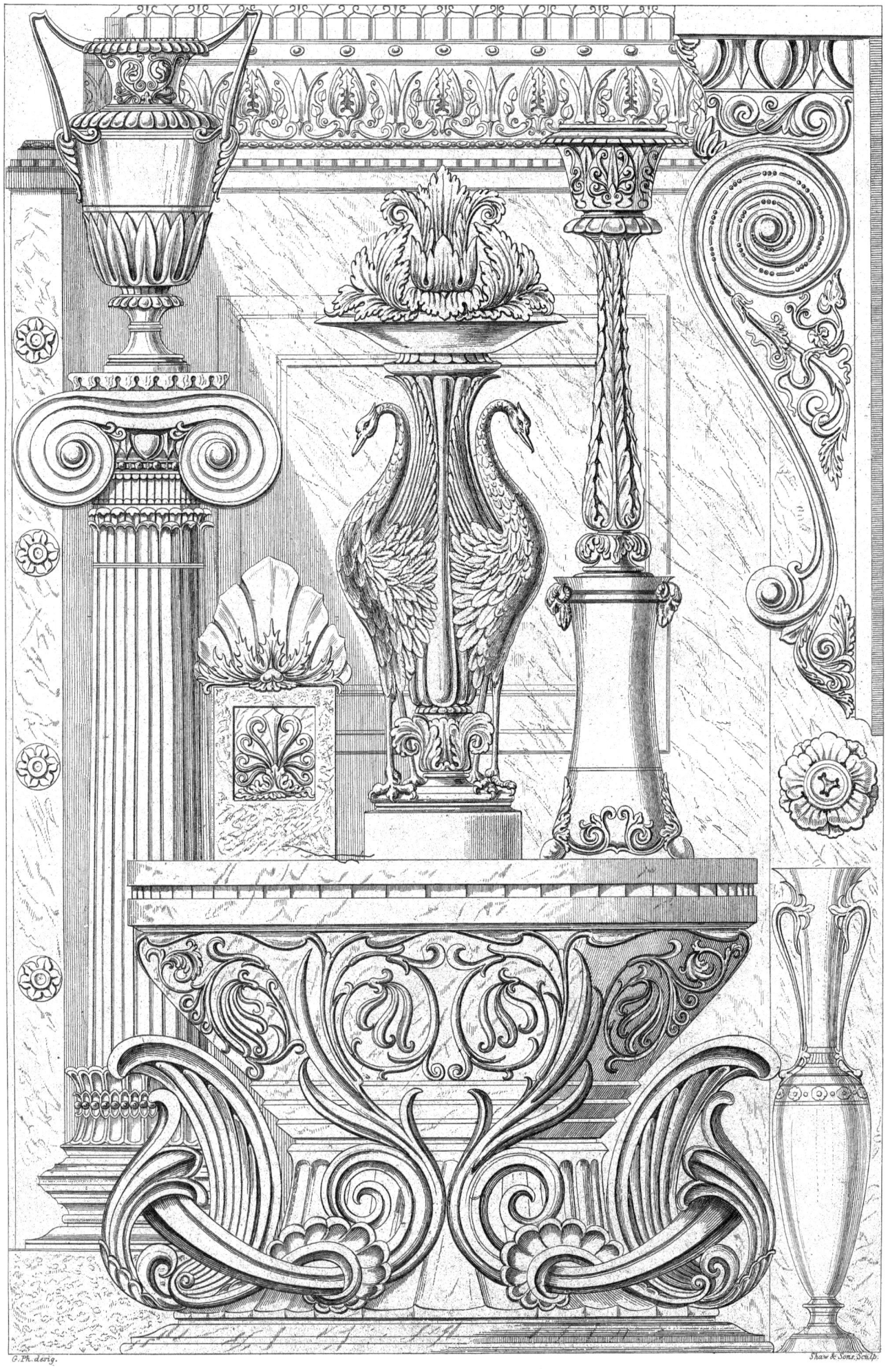

GRECIAN

Shaw & Sons, Sculp.

PLATE 7

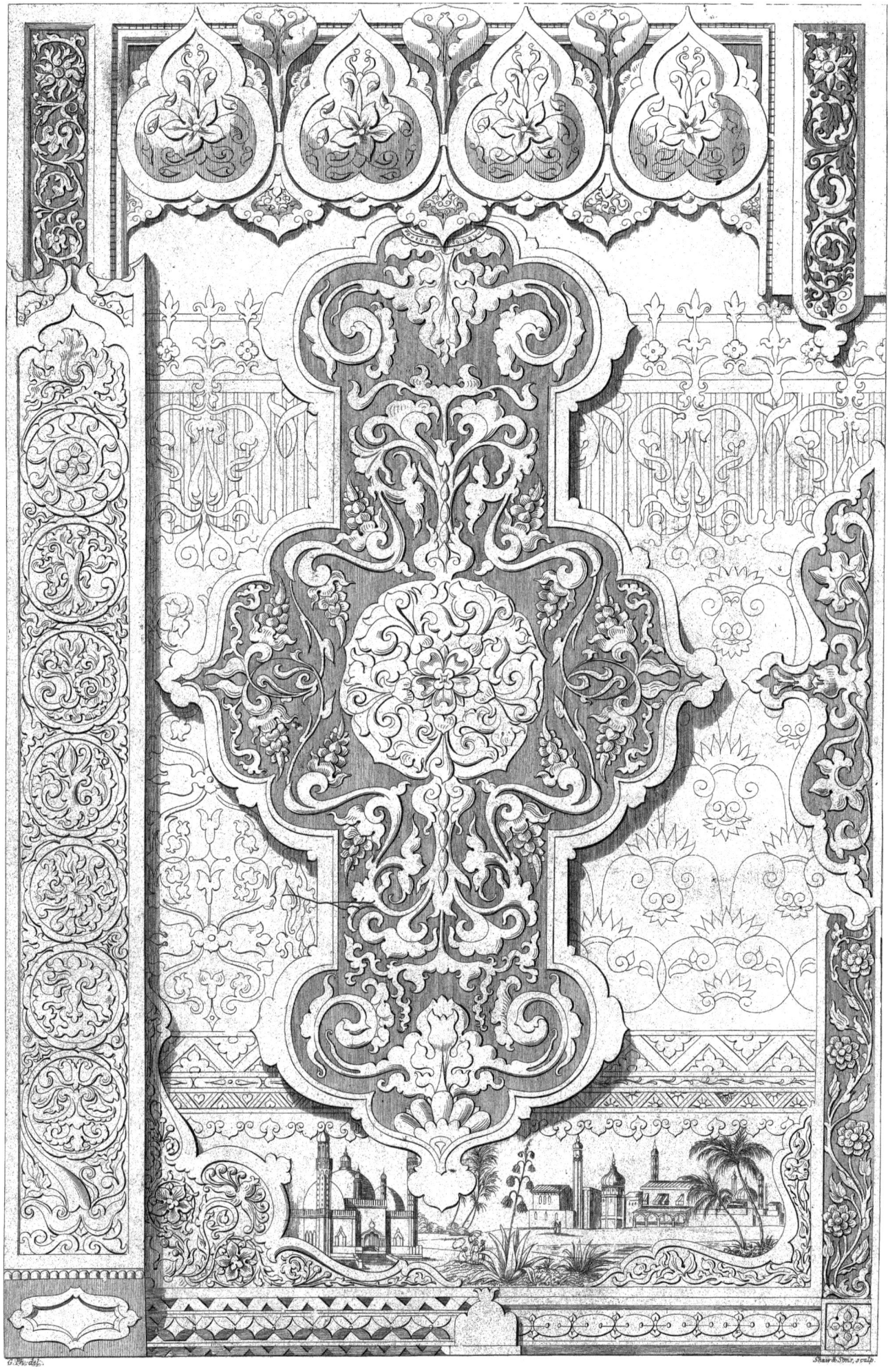

HINDOSTANEE

PLATE 8

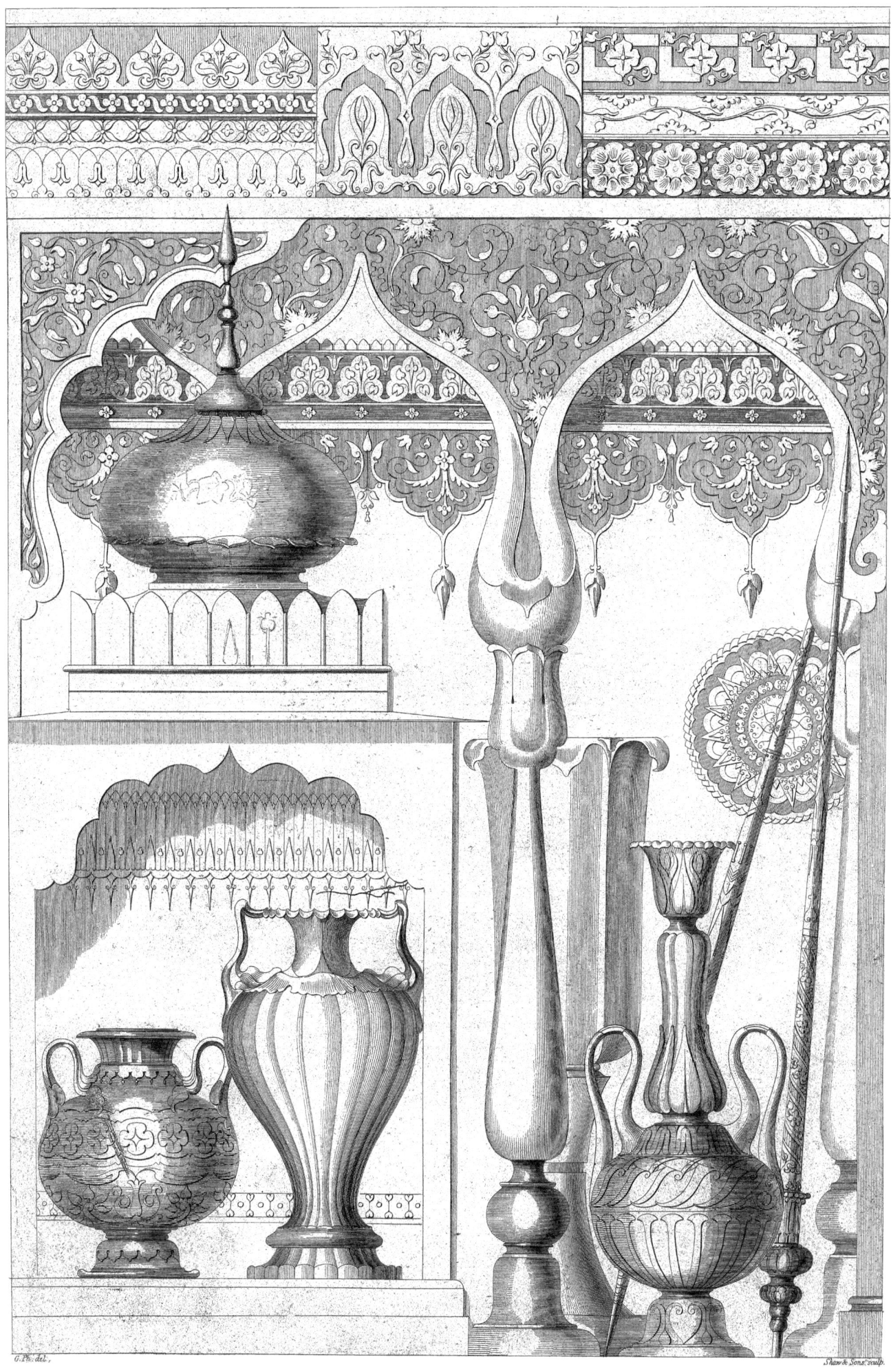

PERSIAN

PLATE 9

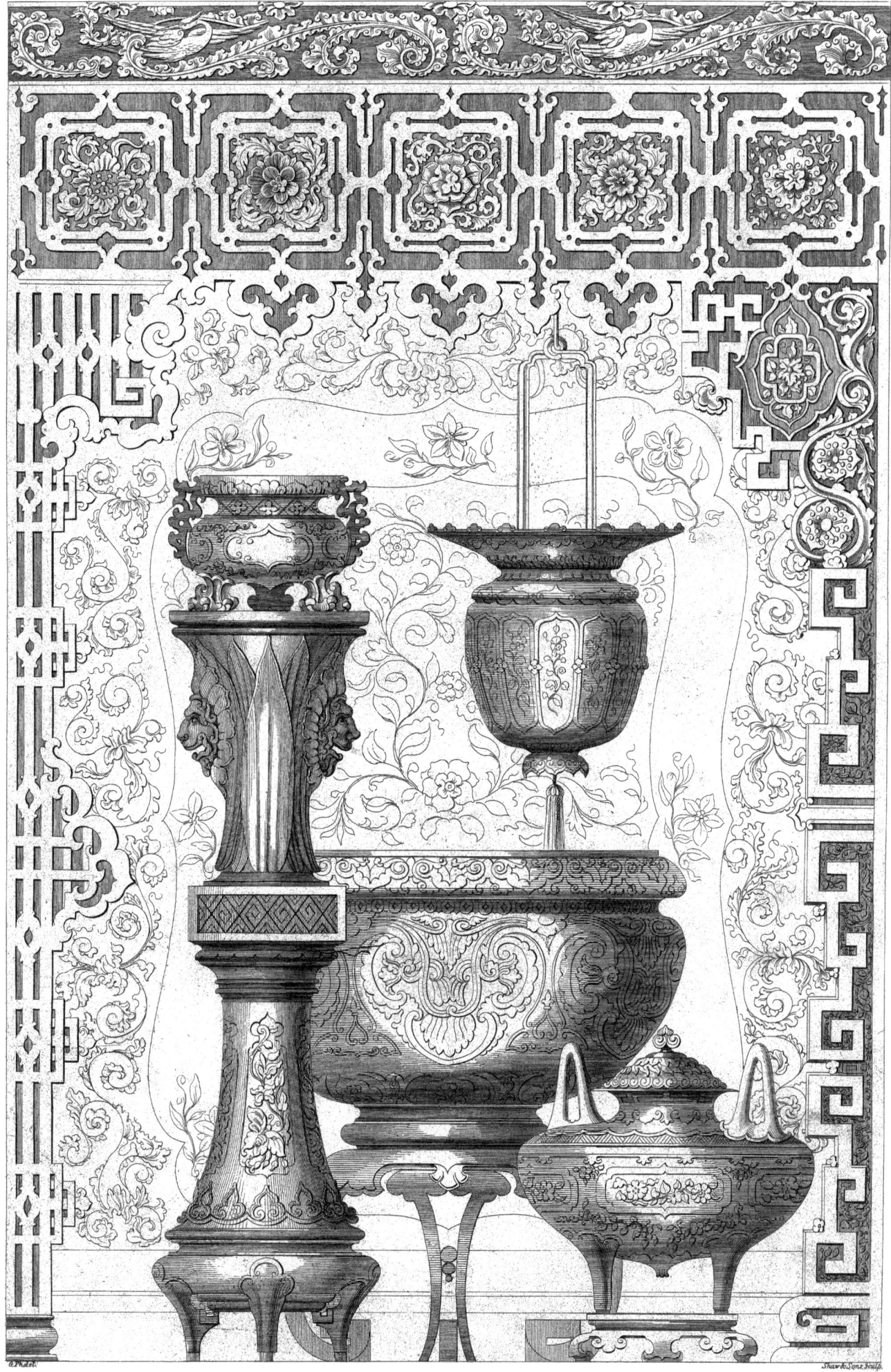

CHINESE

Plate 10

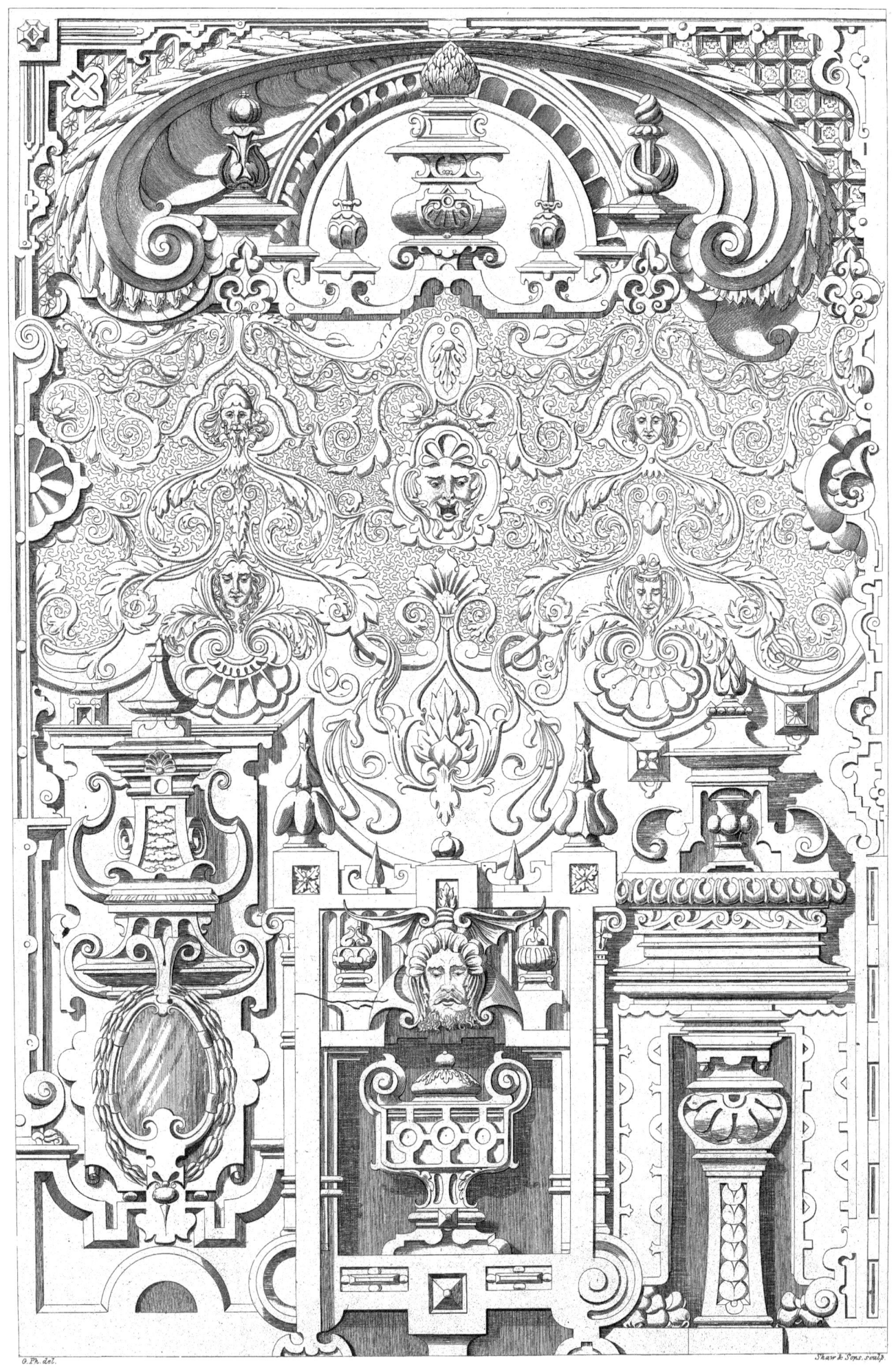

BATAVIAN STYLE OF THE SIXTEENTH CENTURY

PLATE 11

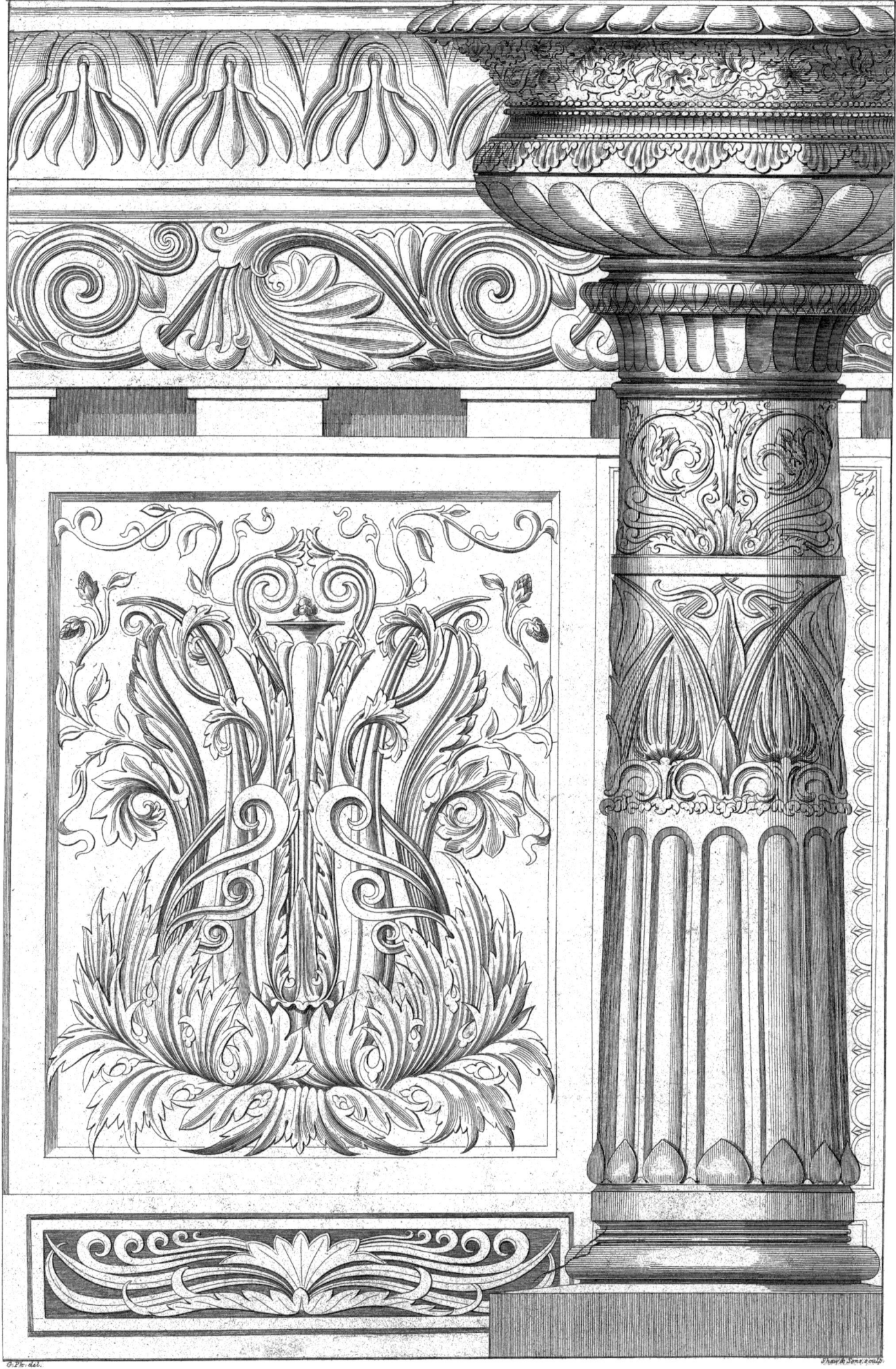

GREEK

PLATE 12

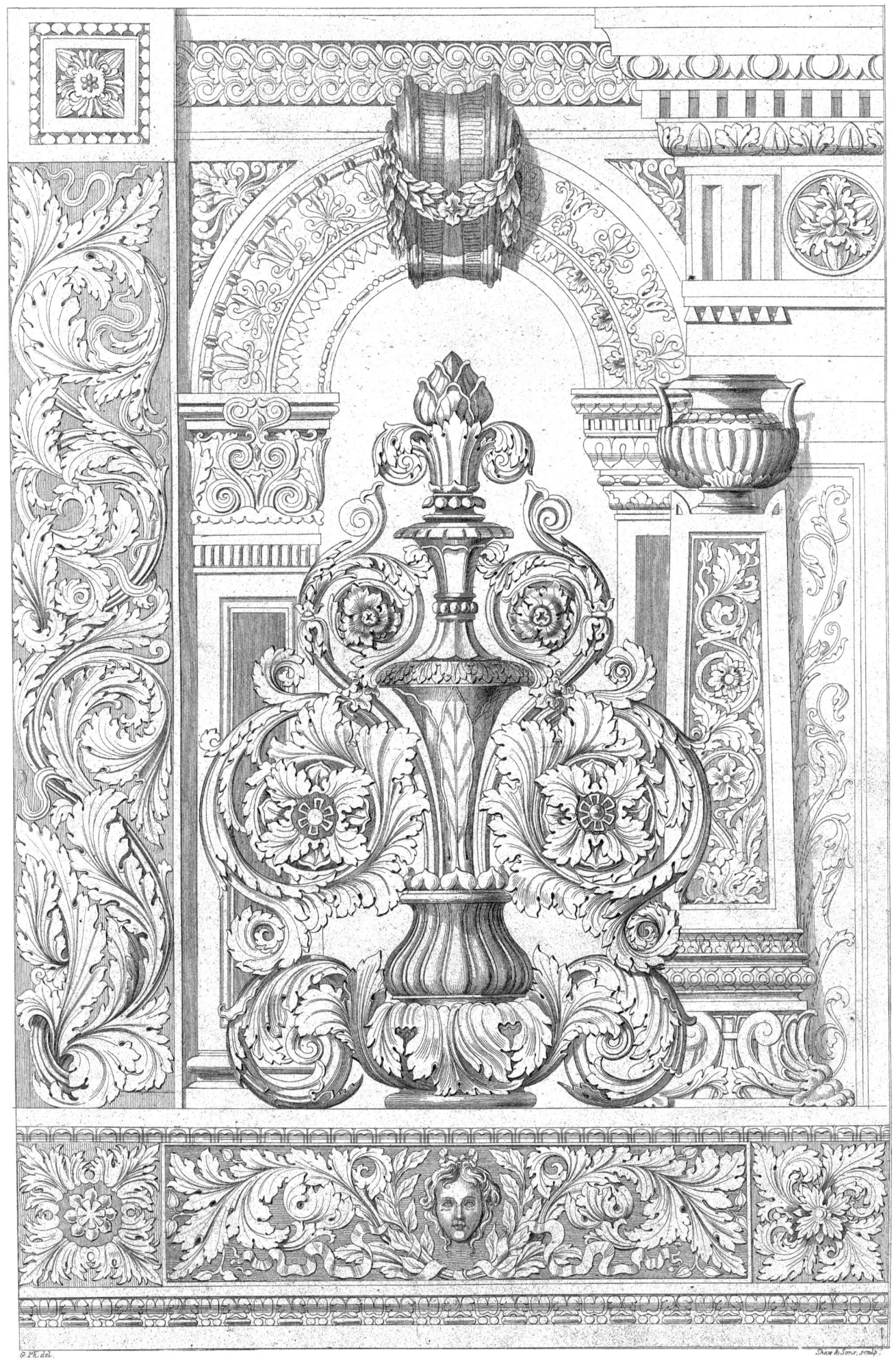

ROMAN

PLATE 13

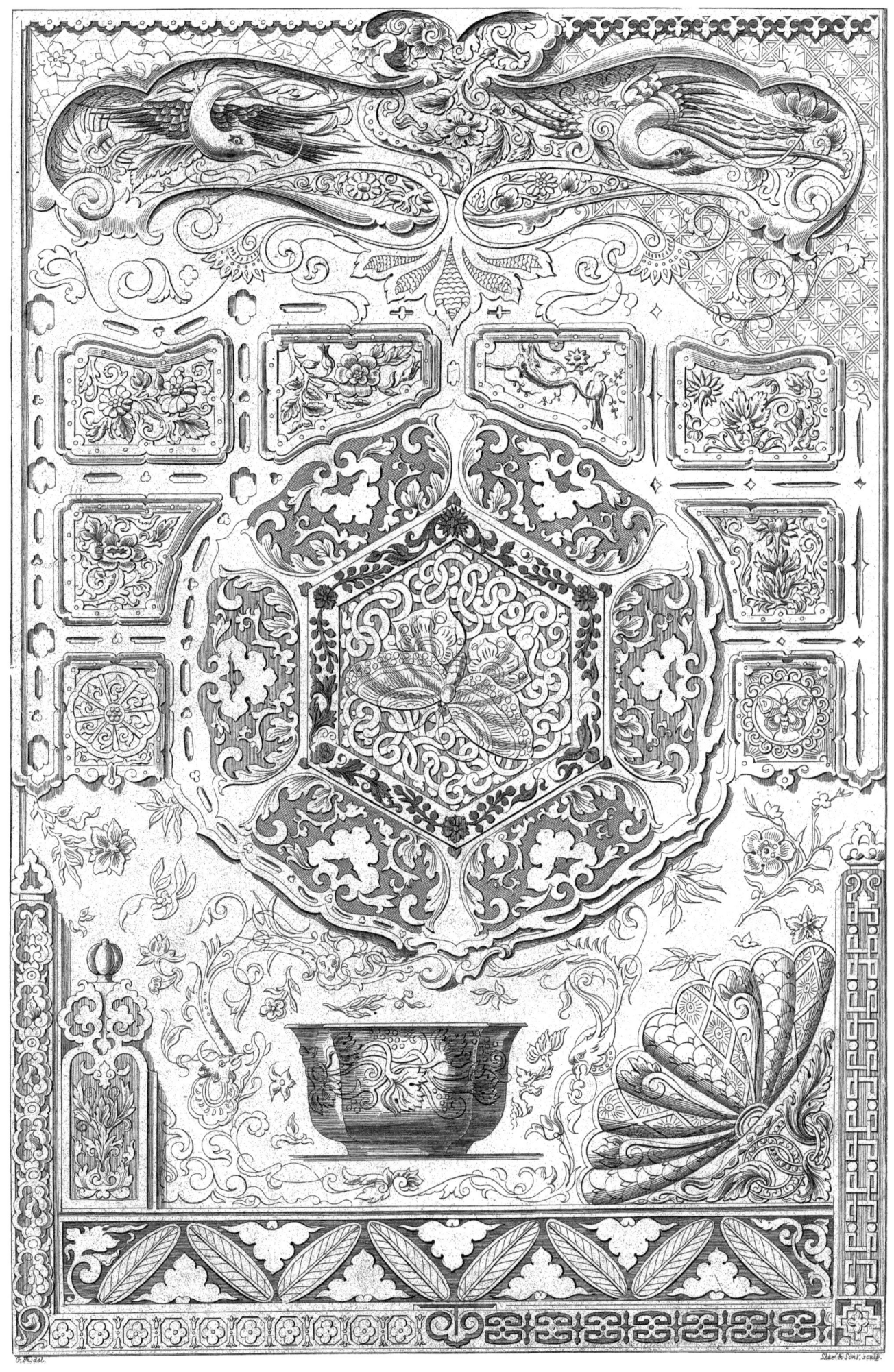

JAPANESE ORNAMENT IN THE CHINESE MANNER

PLATE 14

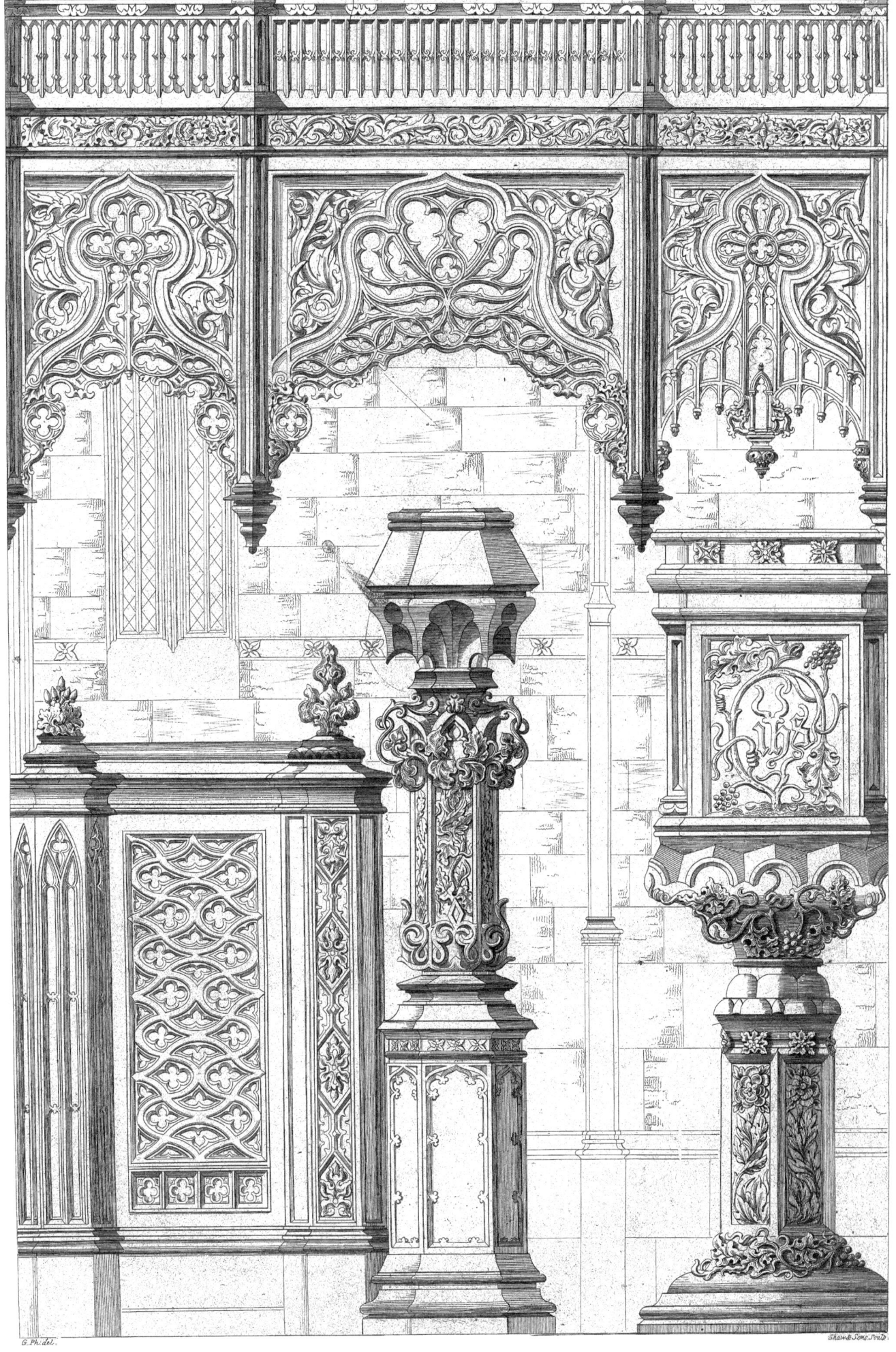

GOTHIC

PLATE 15

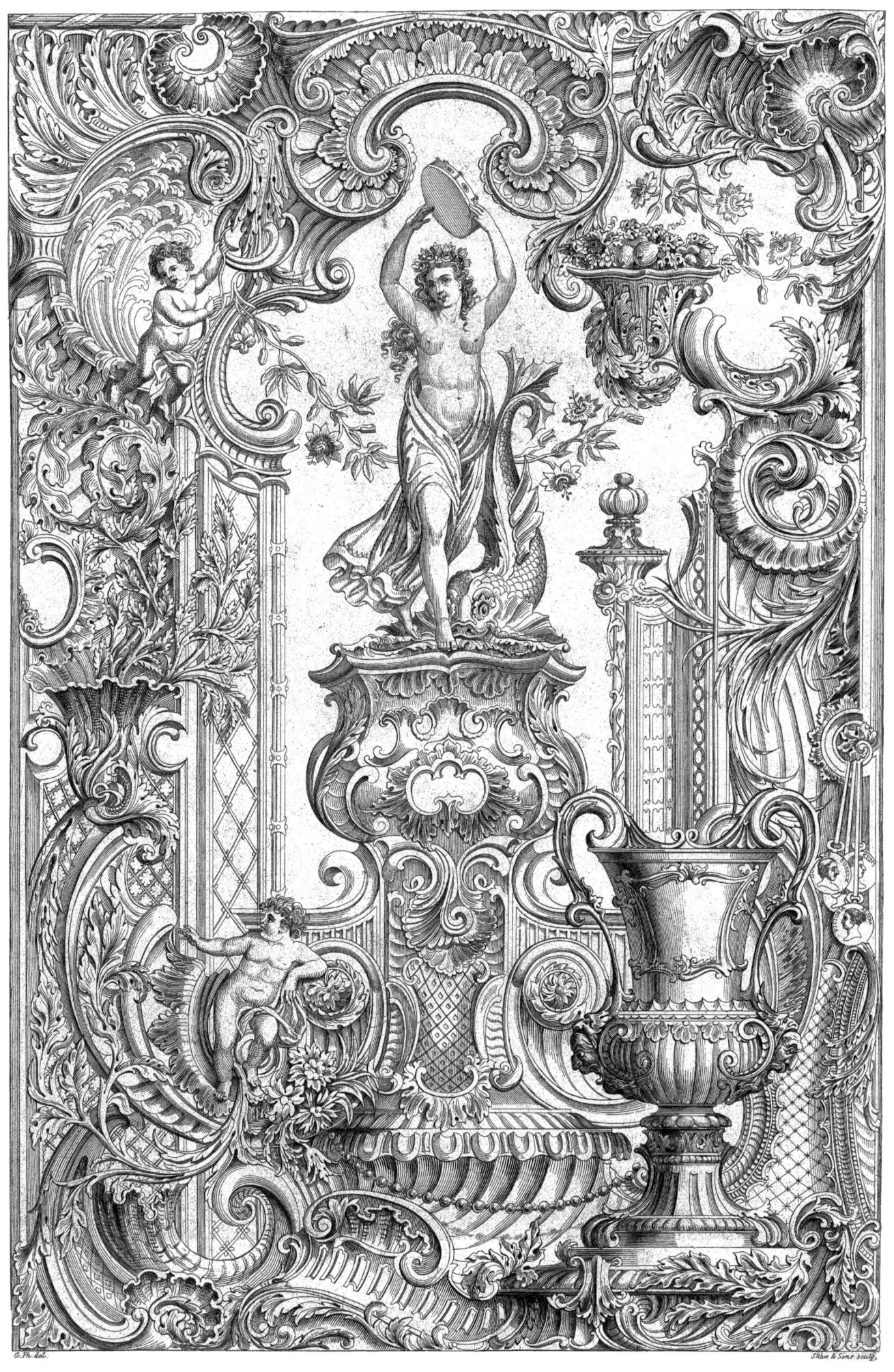

BAROQUE, COMMONLY CALLED LOUIS QUATORZE

PLATE 16

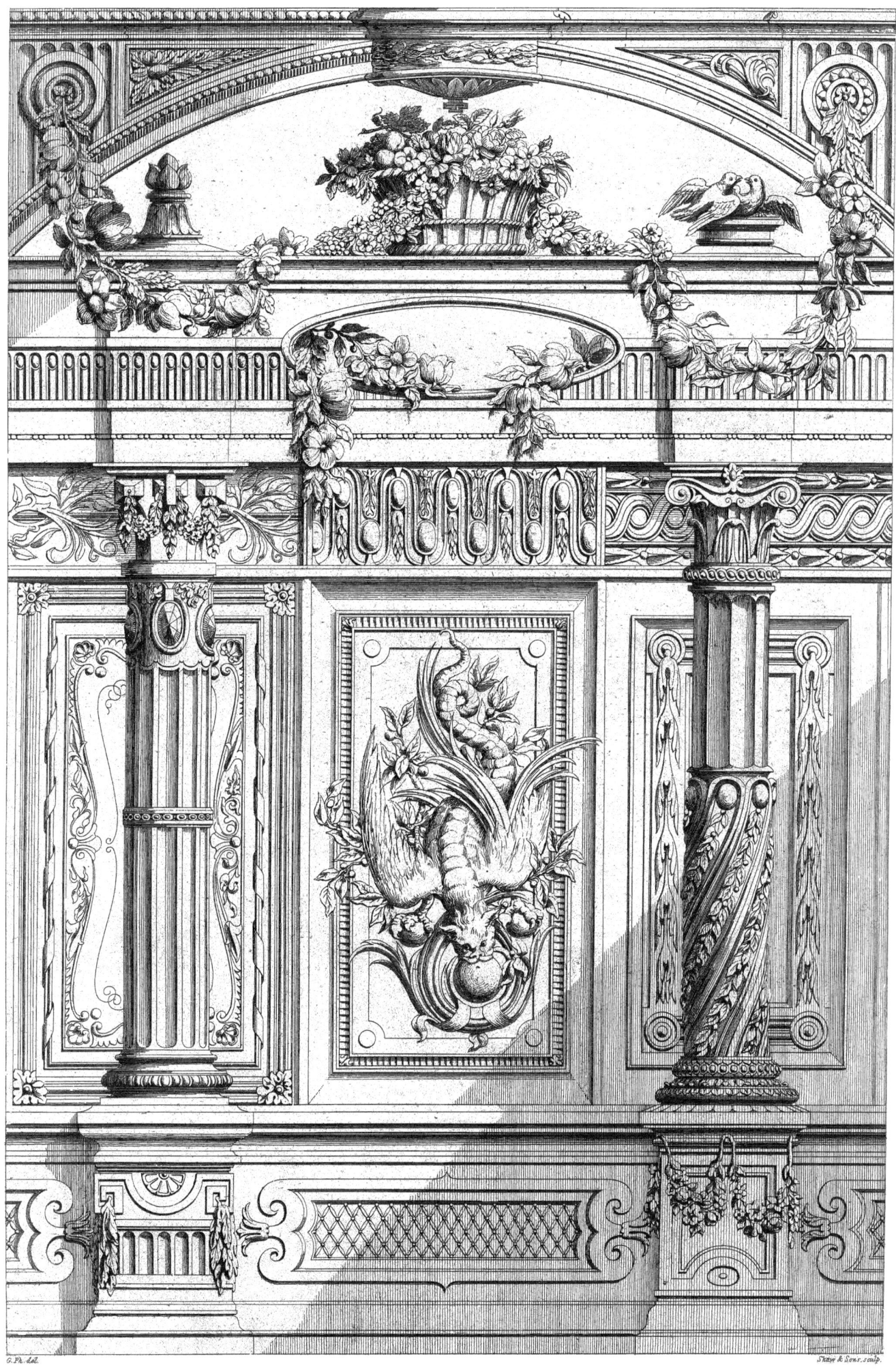

LOUIS QUINZE

PLATE 17

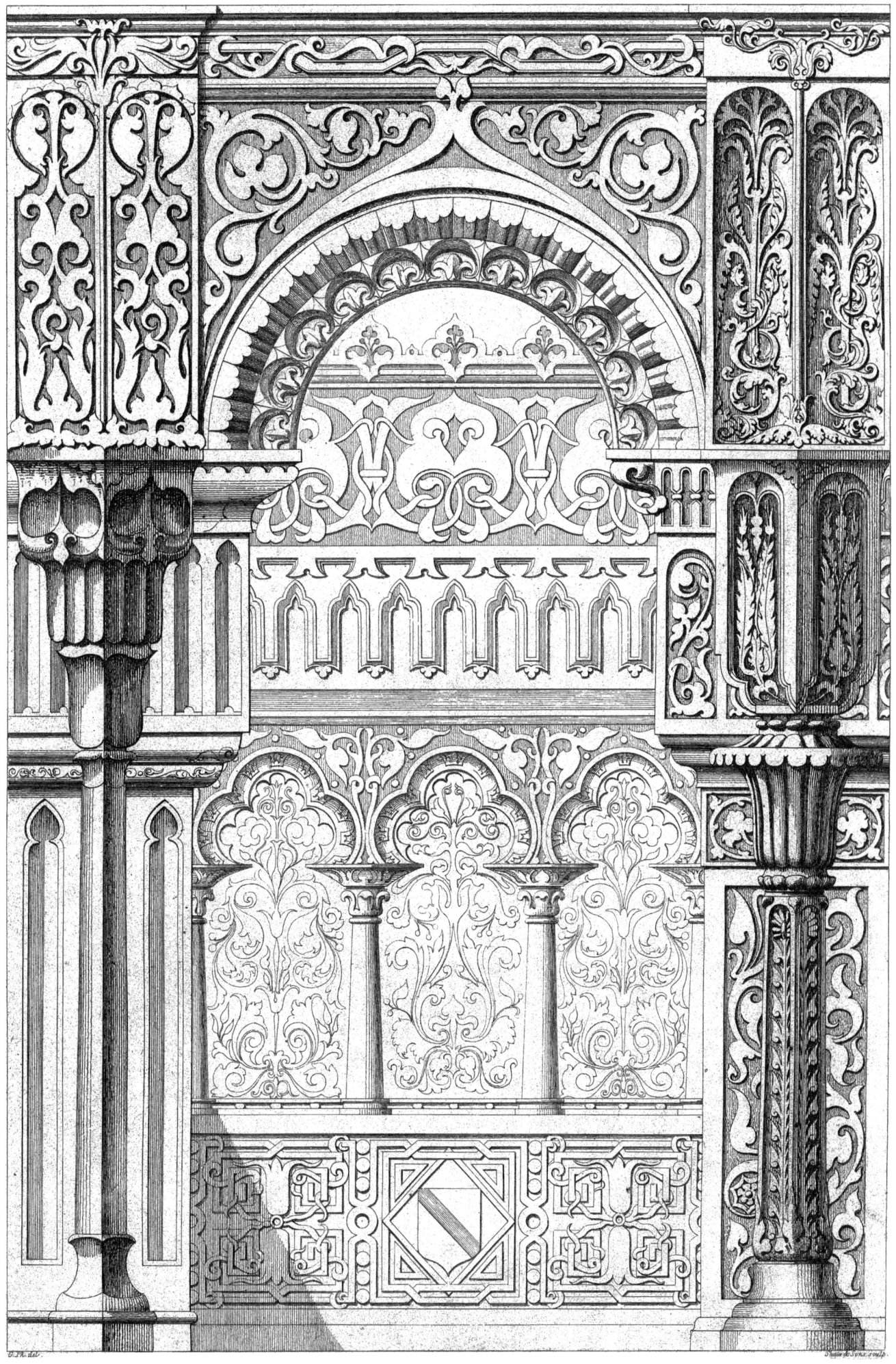

ARABIAN

PLATE 18

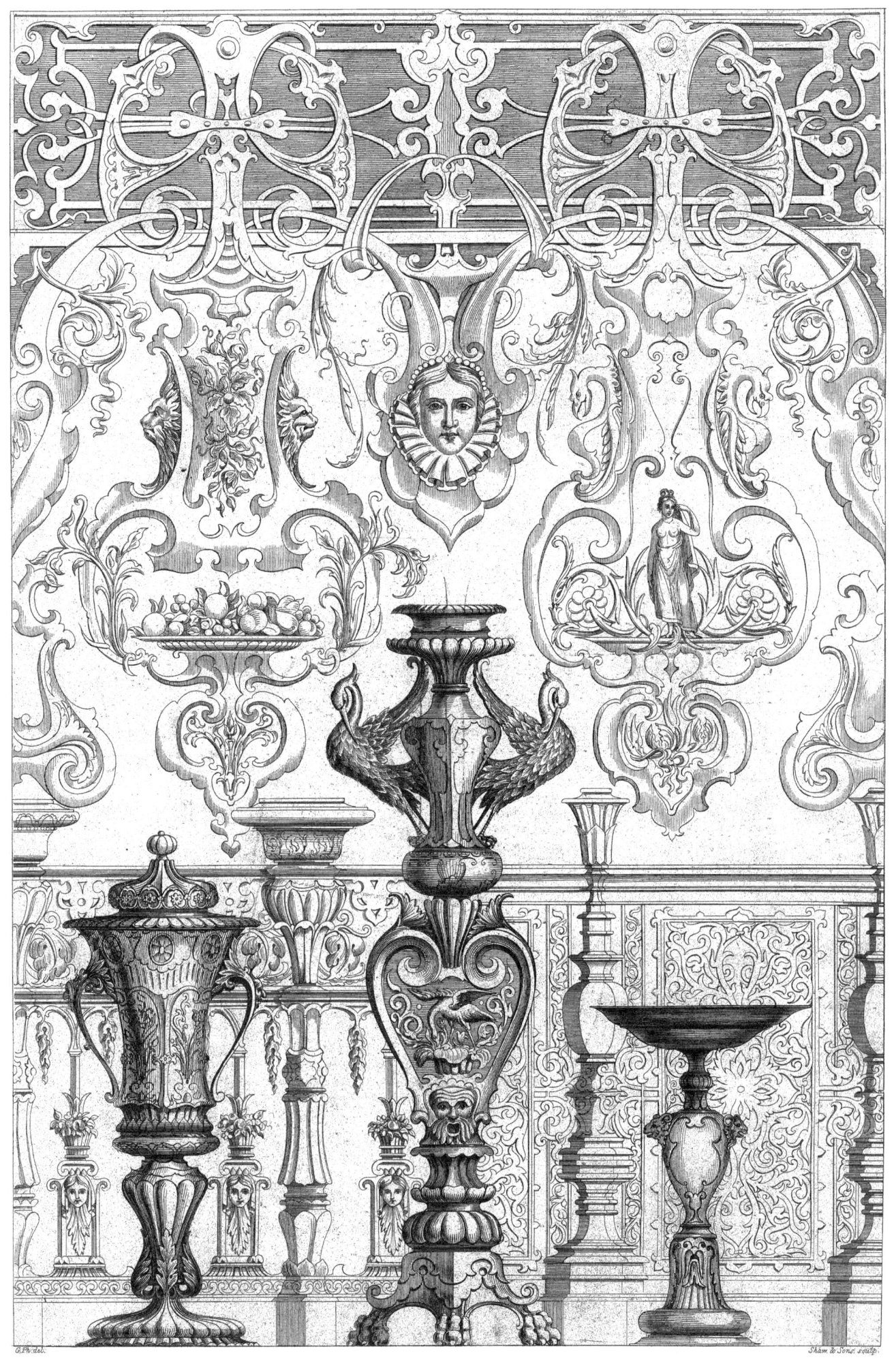

EUROPEAN STYLES OF THE SIXTEENTH CENTURY

PLATE 19

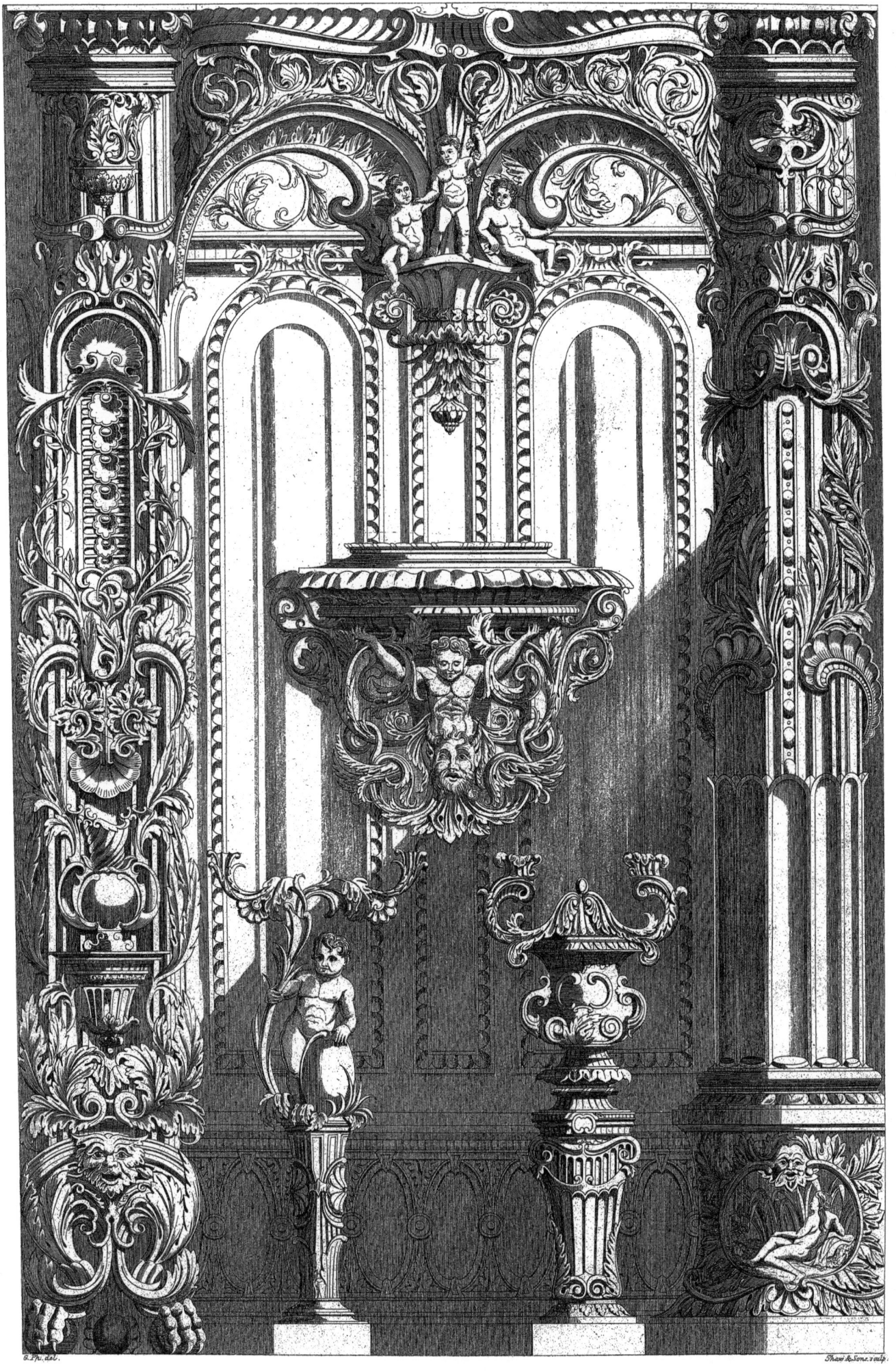

LOUIS QUATORZE

PLATE 20

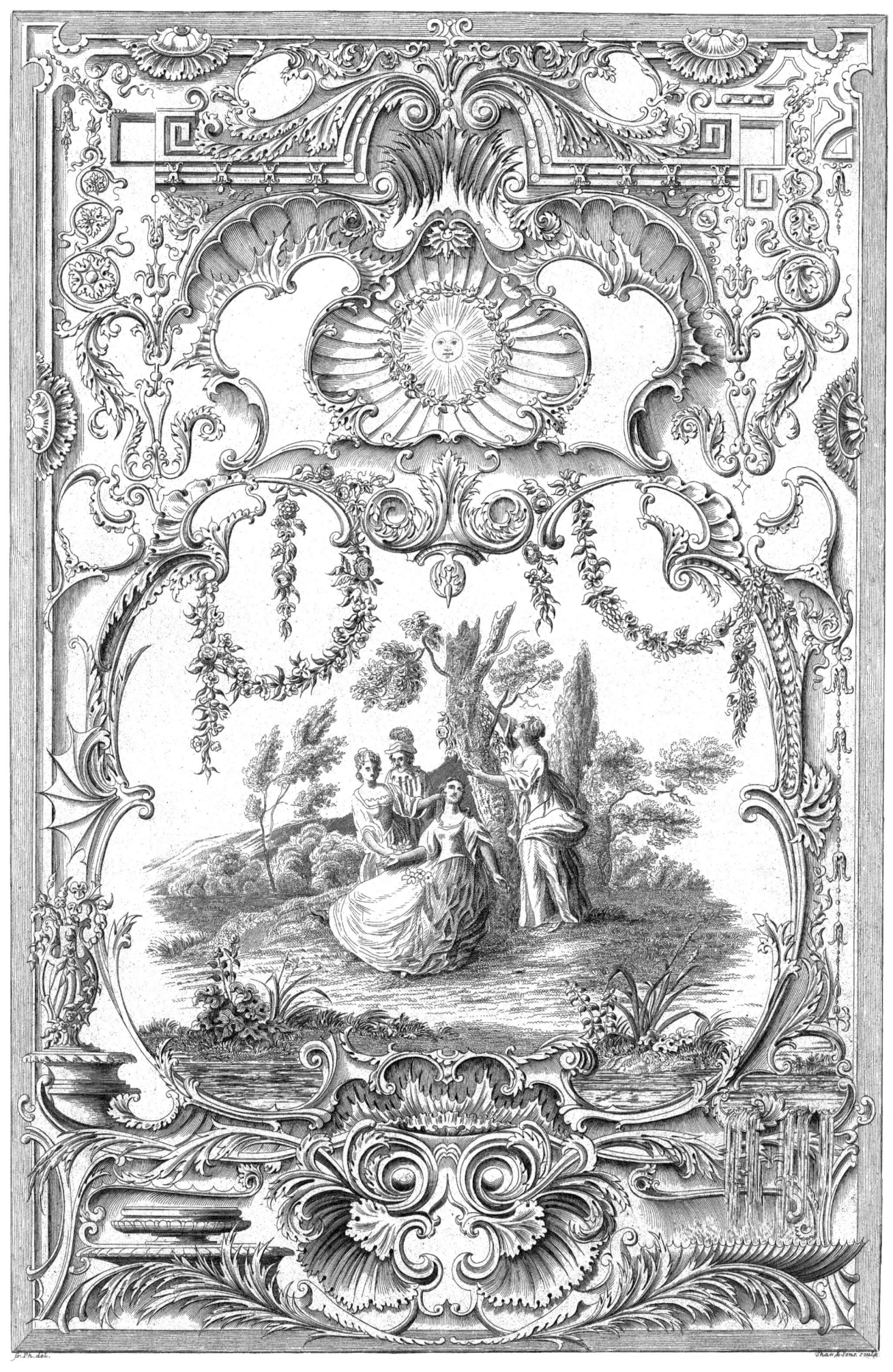

LOUIS QUINZE IN THE MANNER OF WATTEAU

PLATE 21

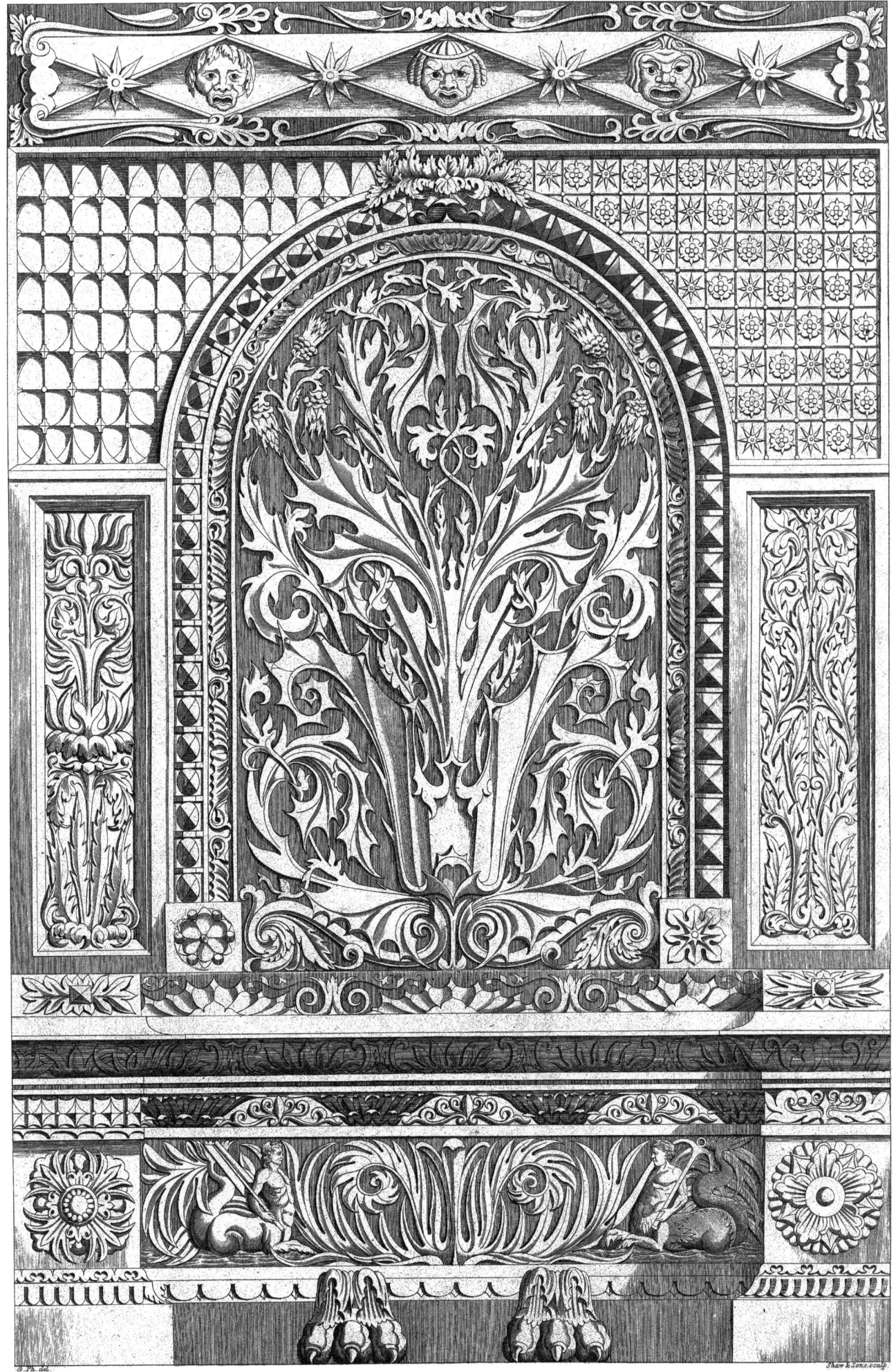

BYZANTINE

PLATE 22

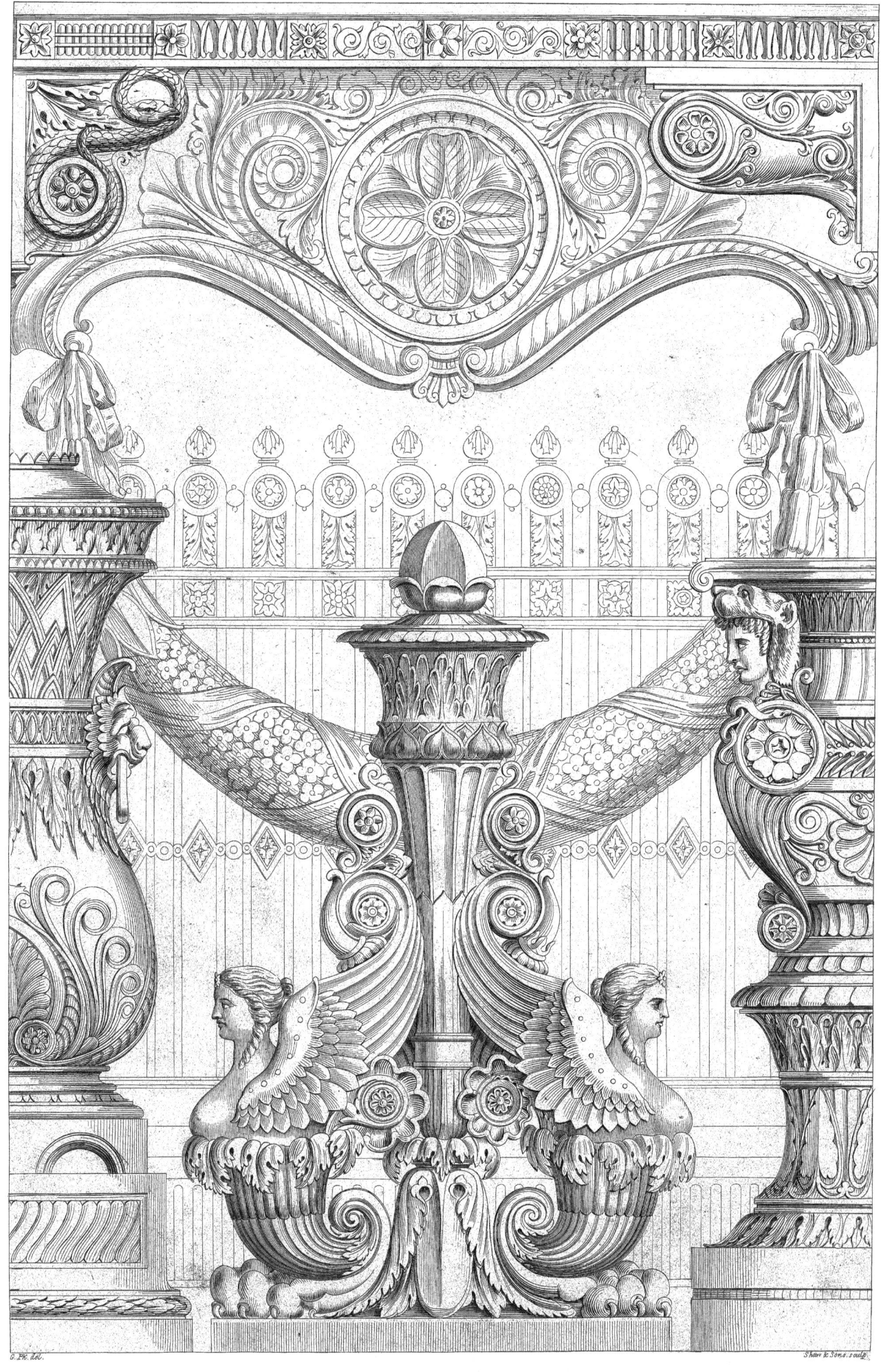

MODERN FRENCH

PLATE 23

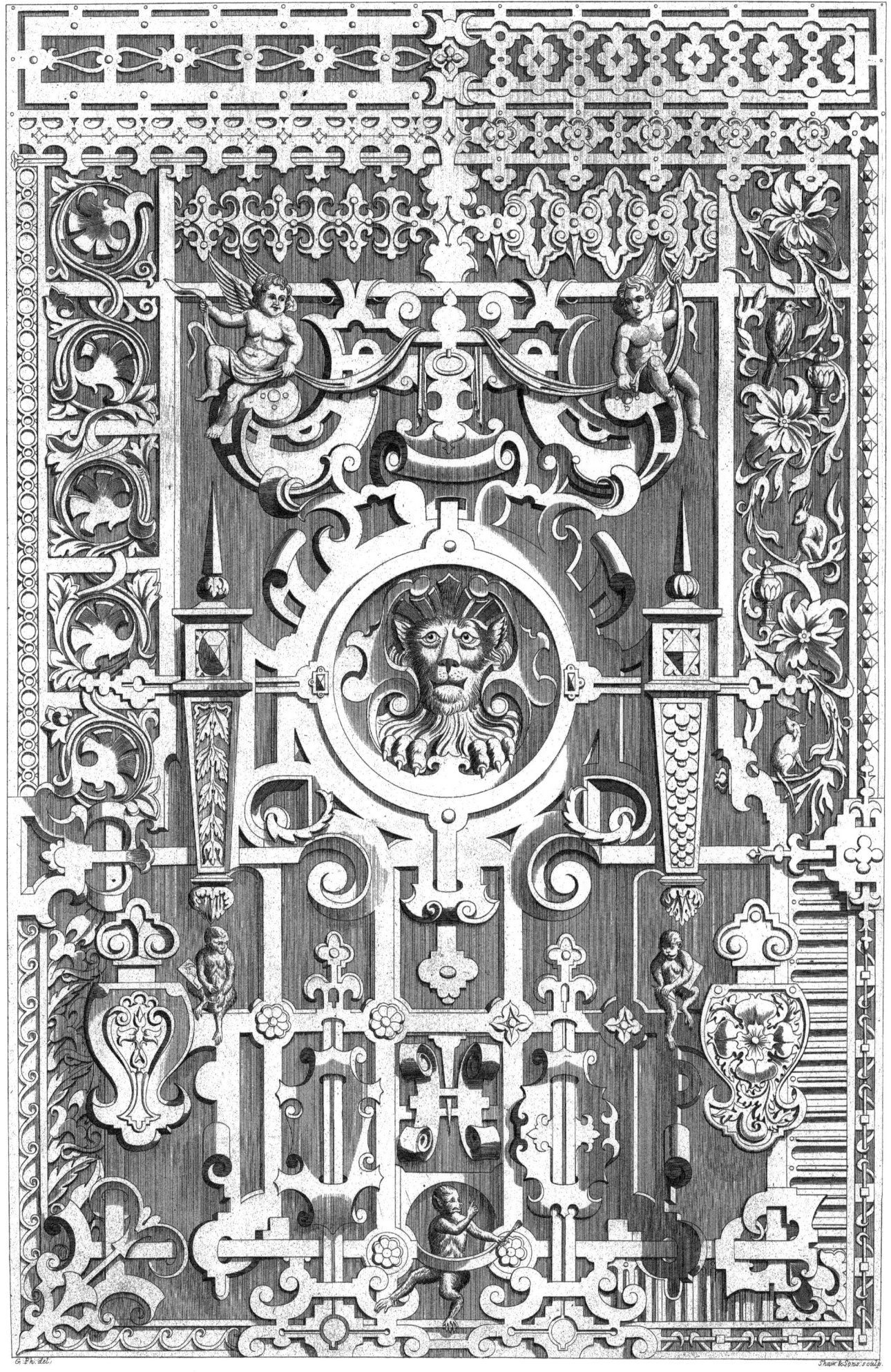

BOLTED ELIZABETHAN

PLATE 24

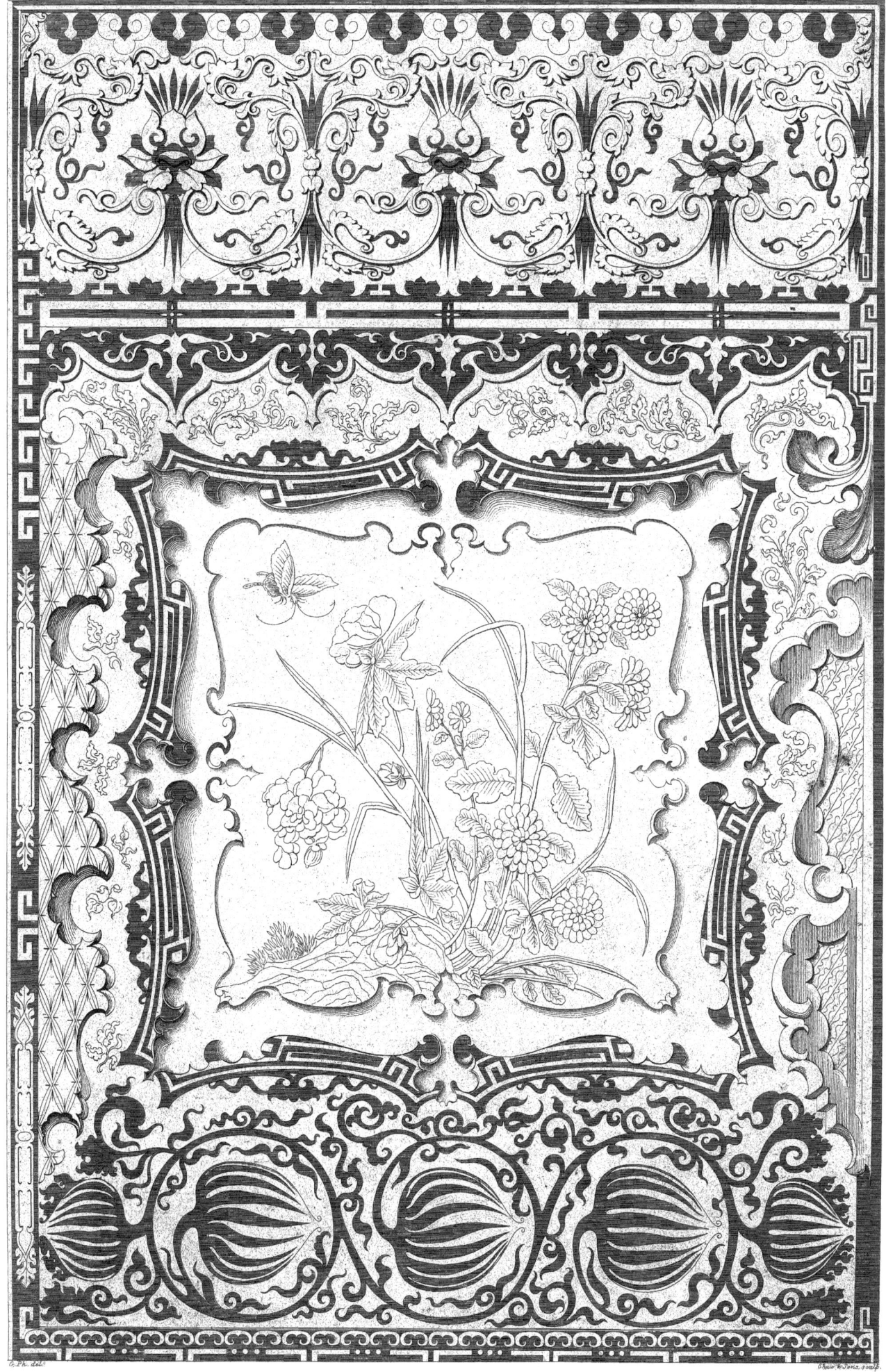

CHINESE

PLATE 25

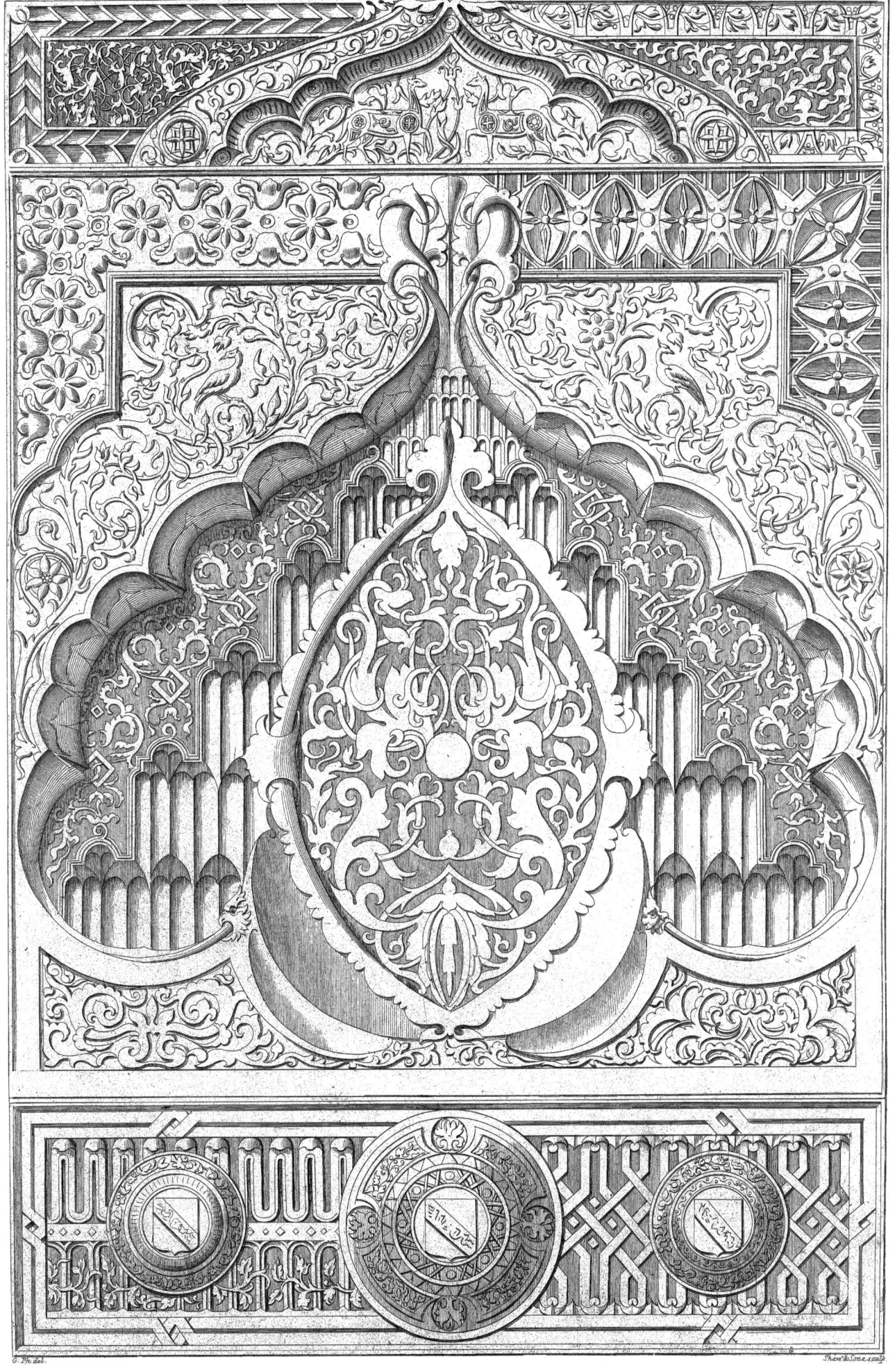

ARABIAN

PLATE 26

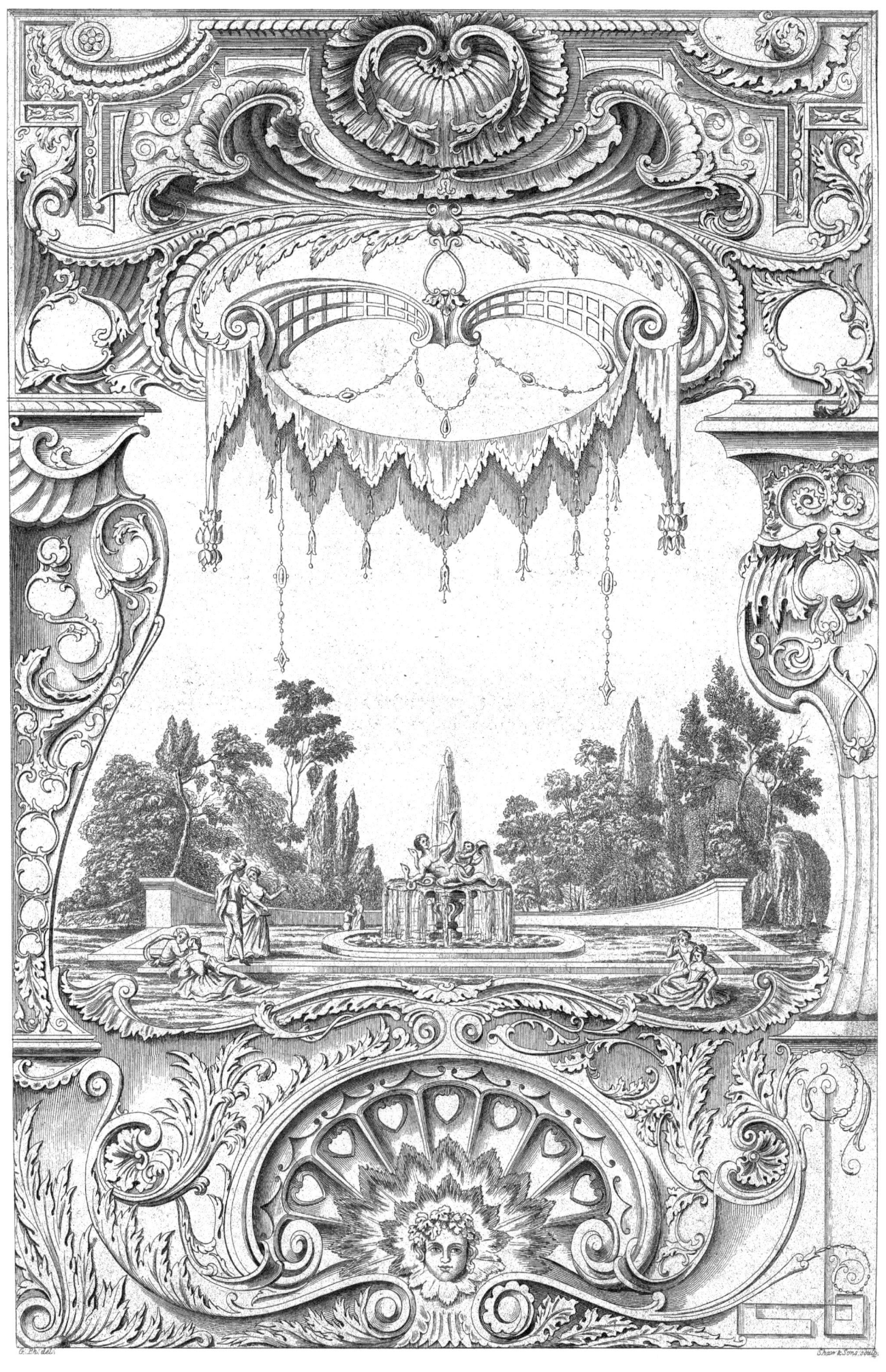

LOUIS QUINZE IN THE MANNER OF WATTEAU

PLATE 27

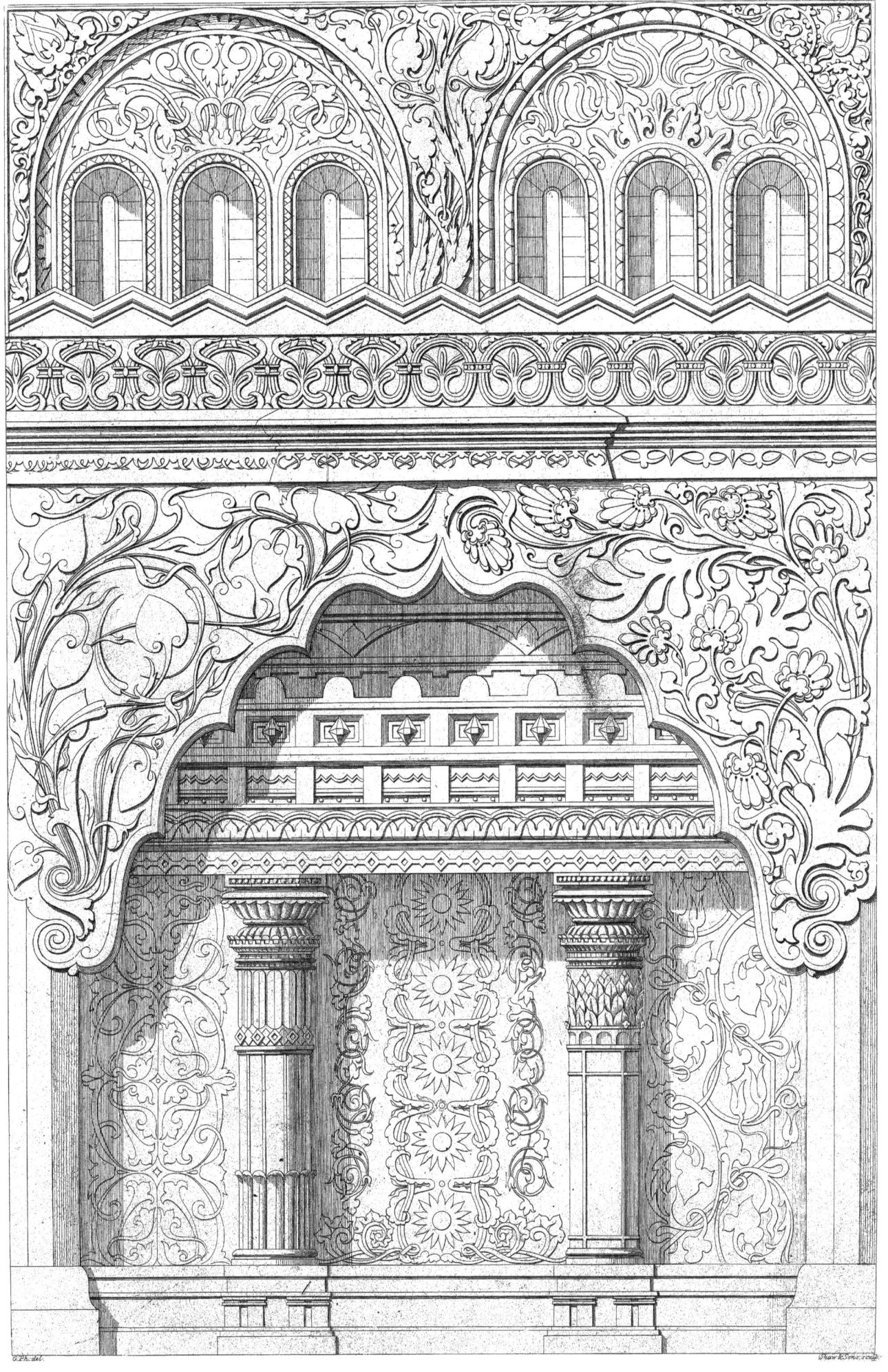

BYZANTINE

PLATE 28

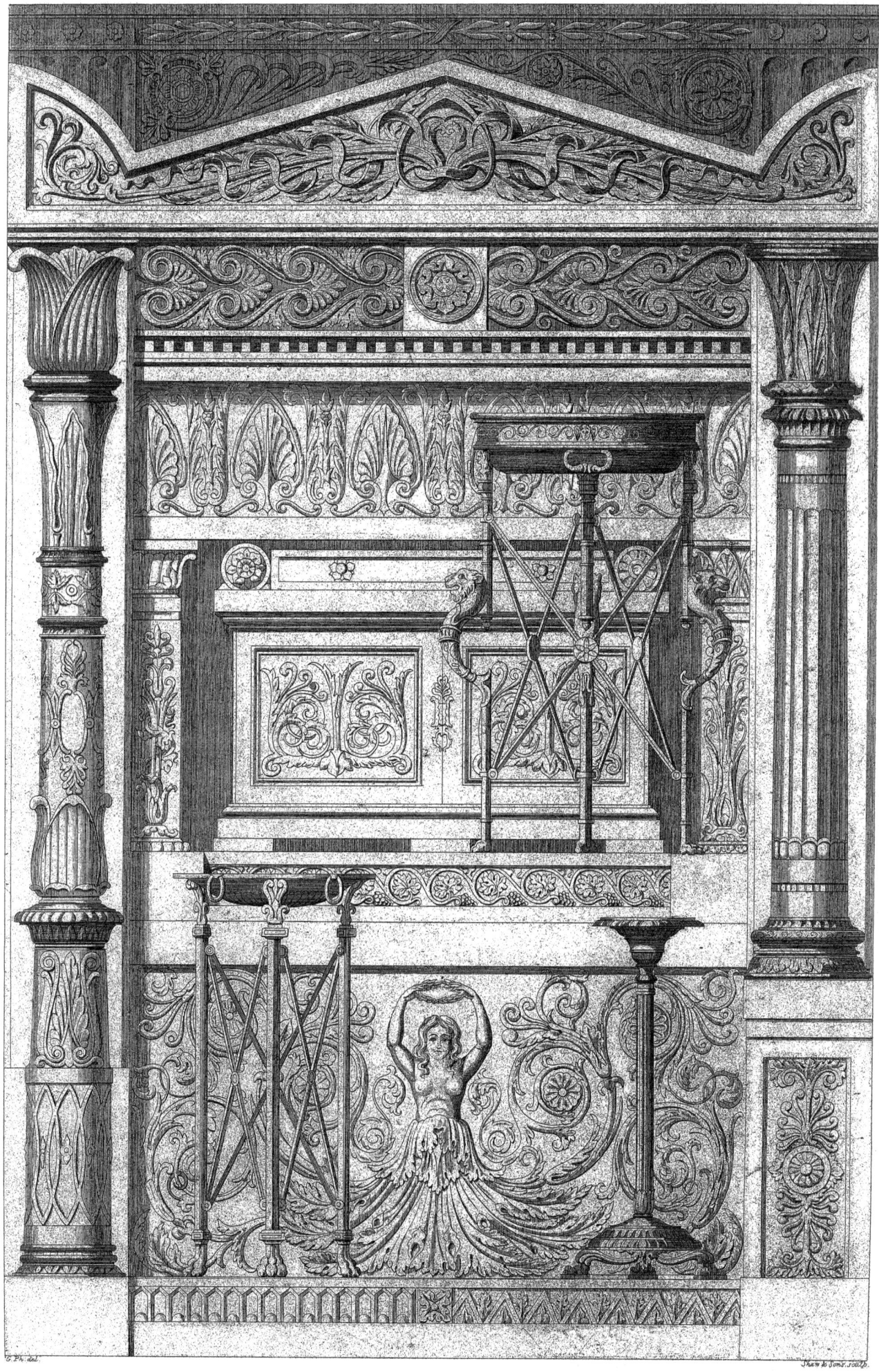

MODERN FRENCH

Plate 29

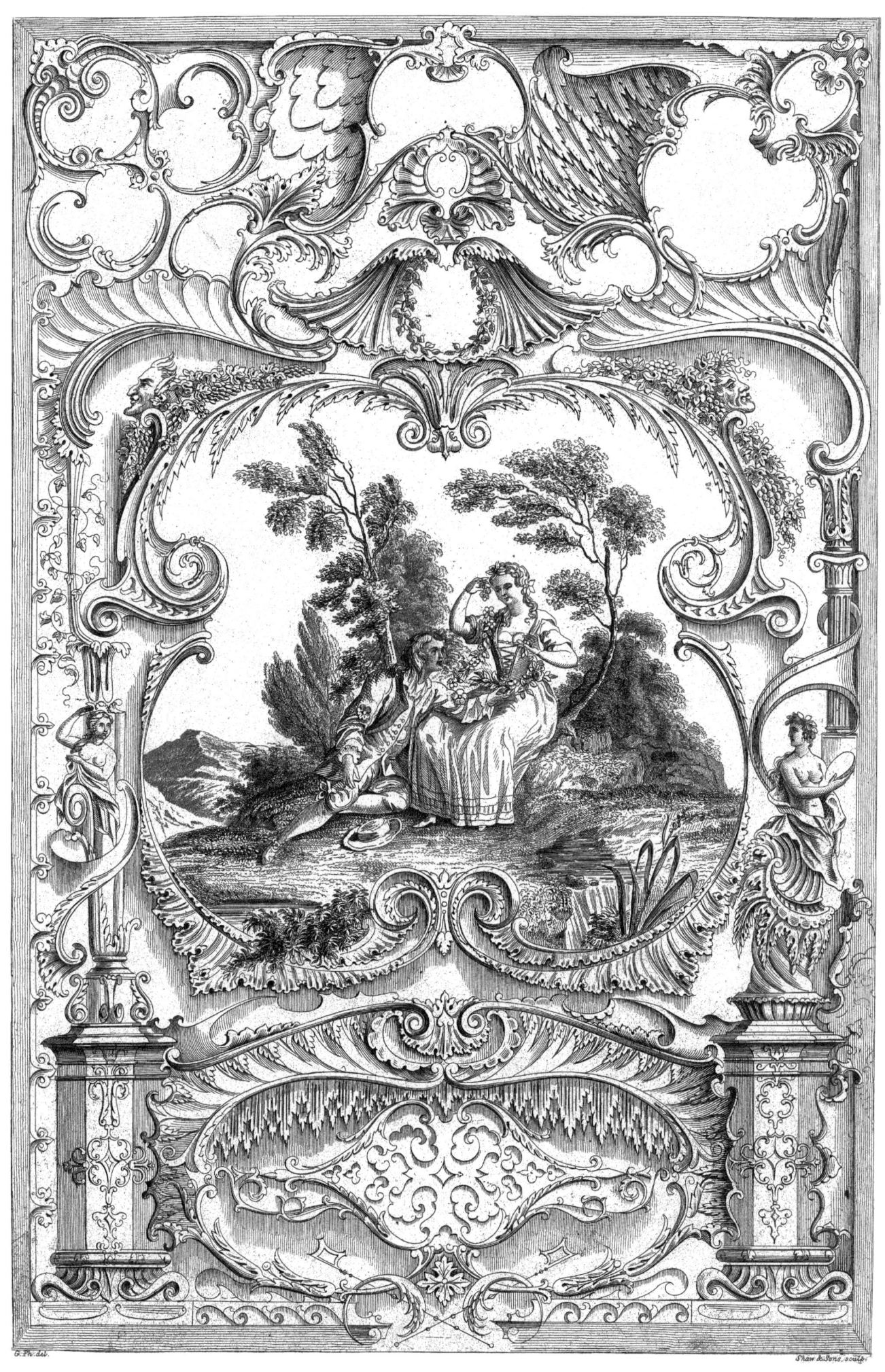

BAROQUE IN THE MANNER OF WATTEAU. SIÈCLE DE LOUIS XV.

PLATE 30

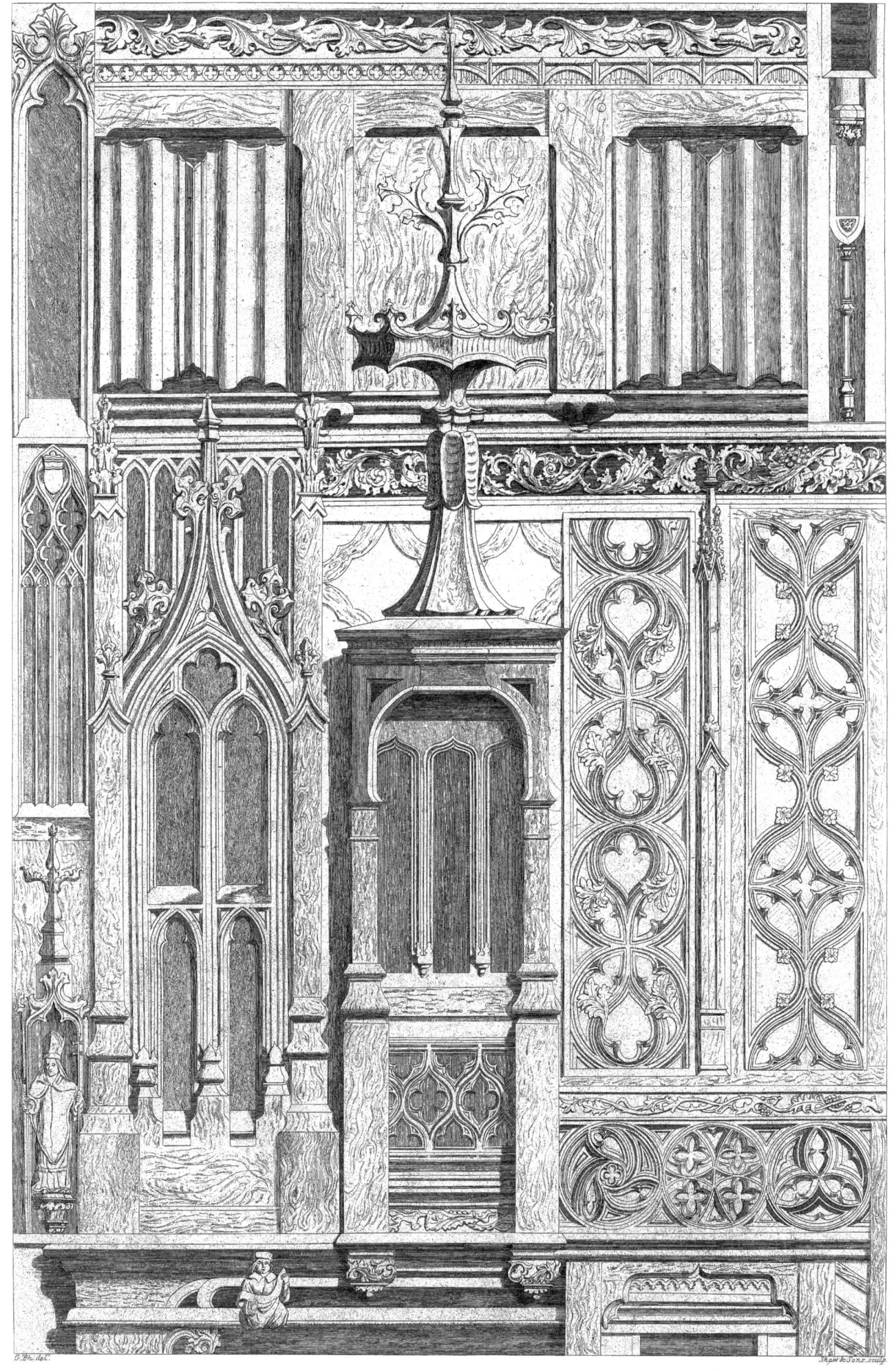

FRENCH TIMBER GOTHIC

PLATE 31

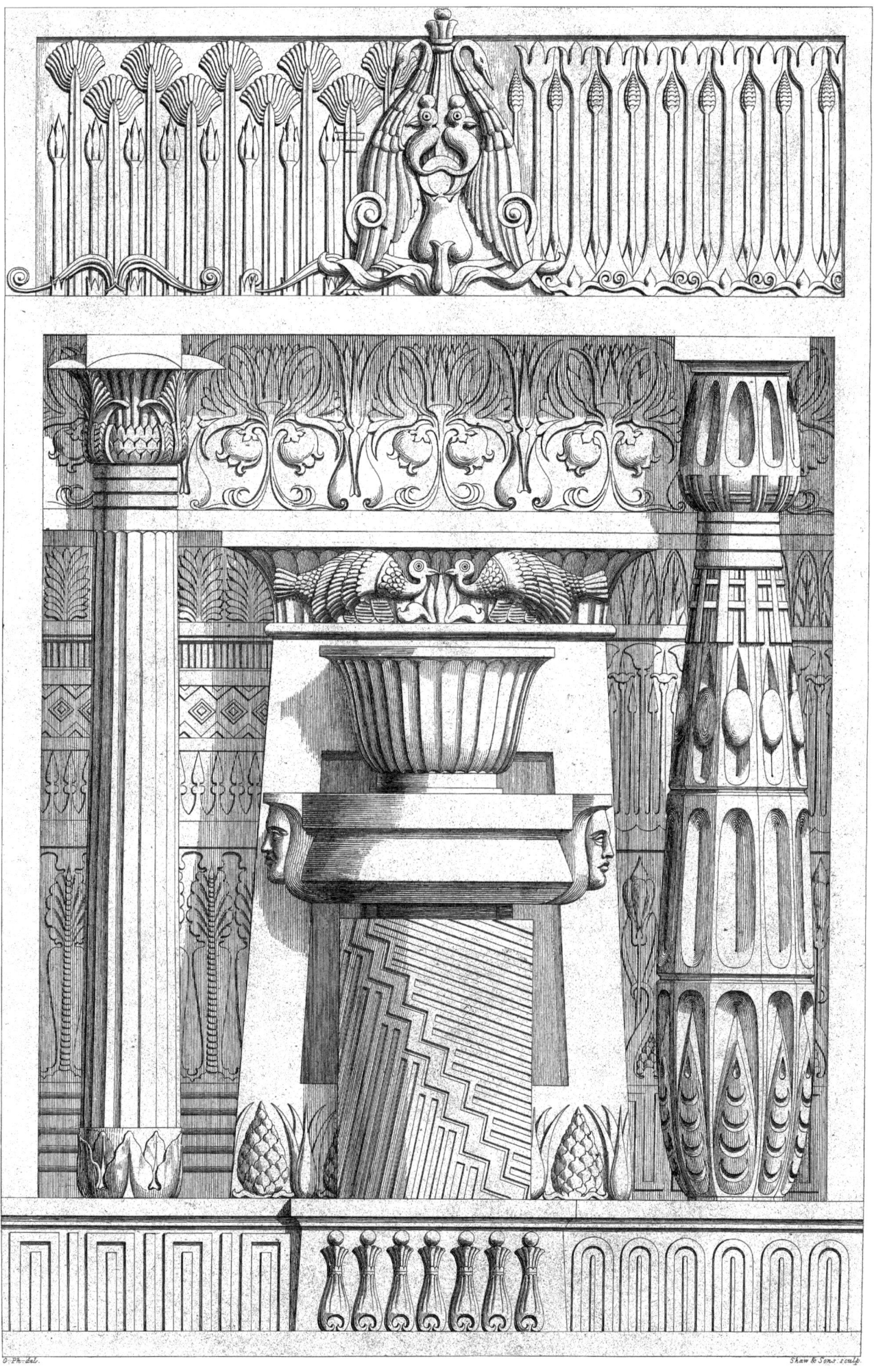

EGYPTIAN

PLATE 32

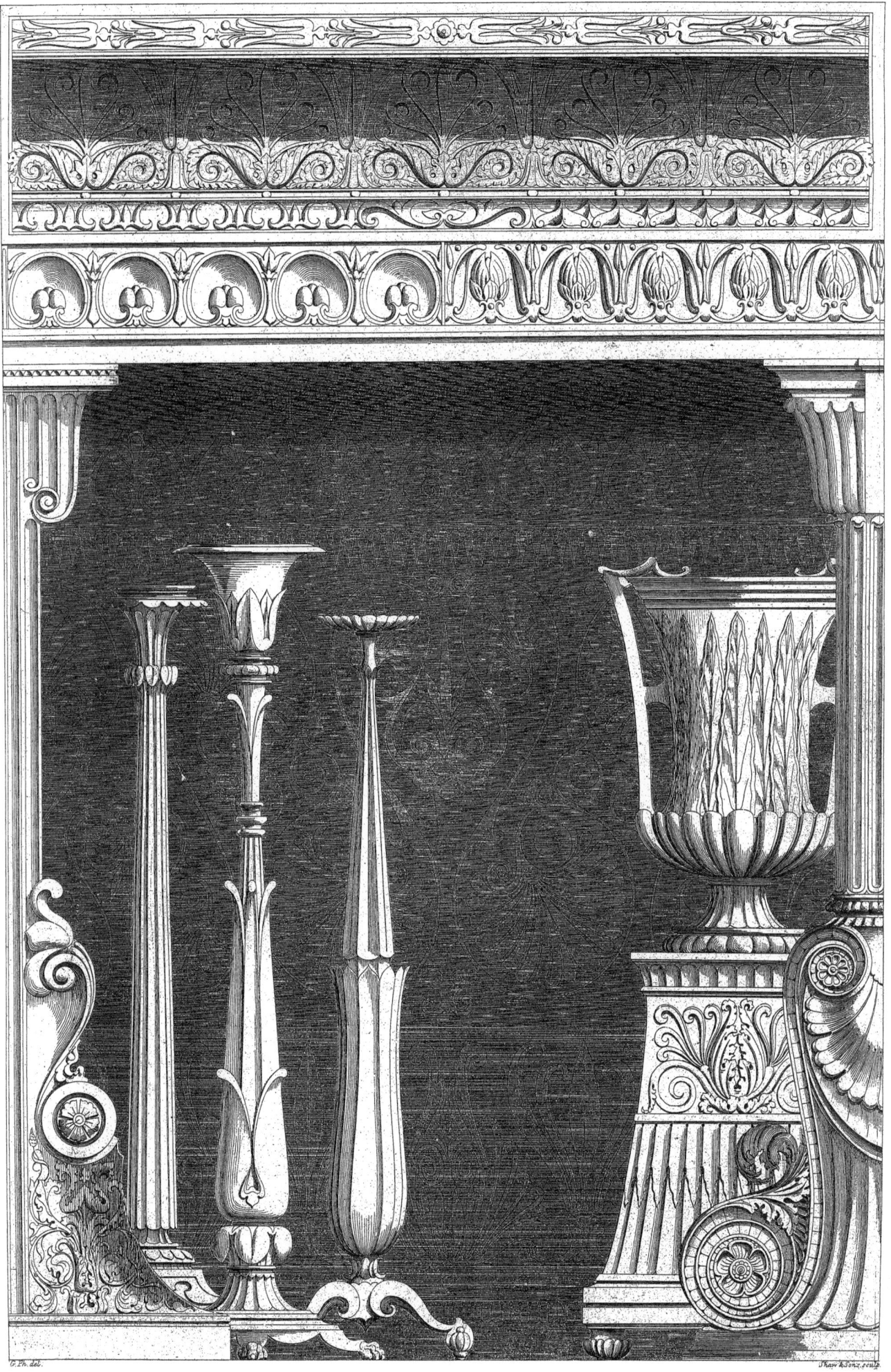

GREEK

PLATE 33

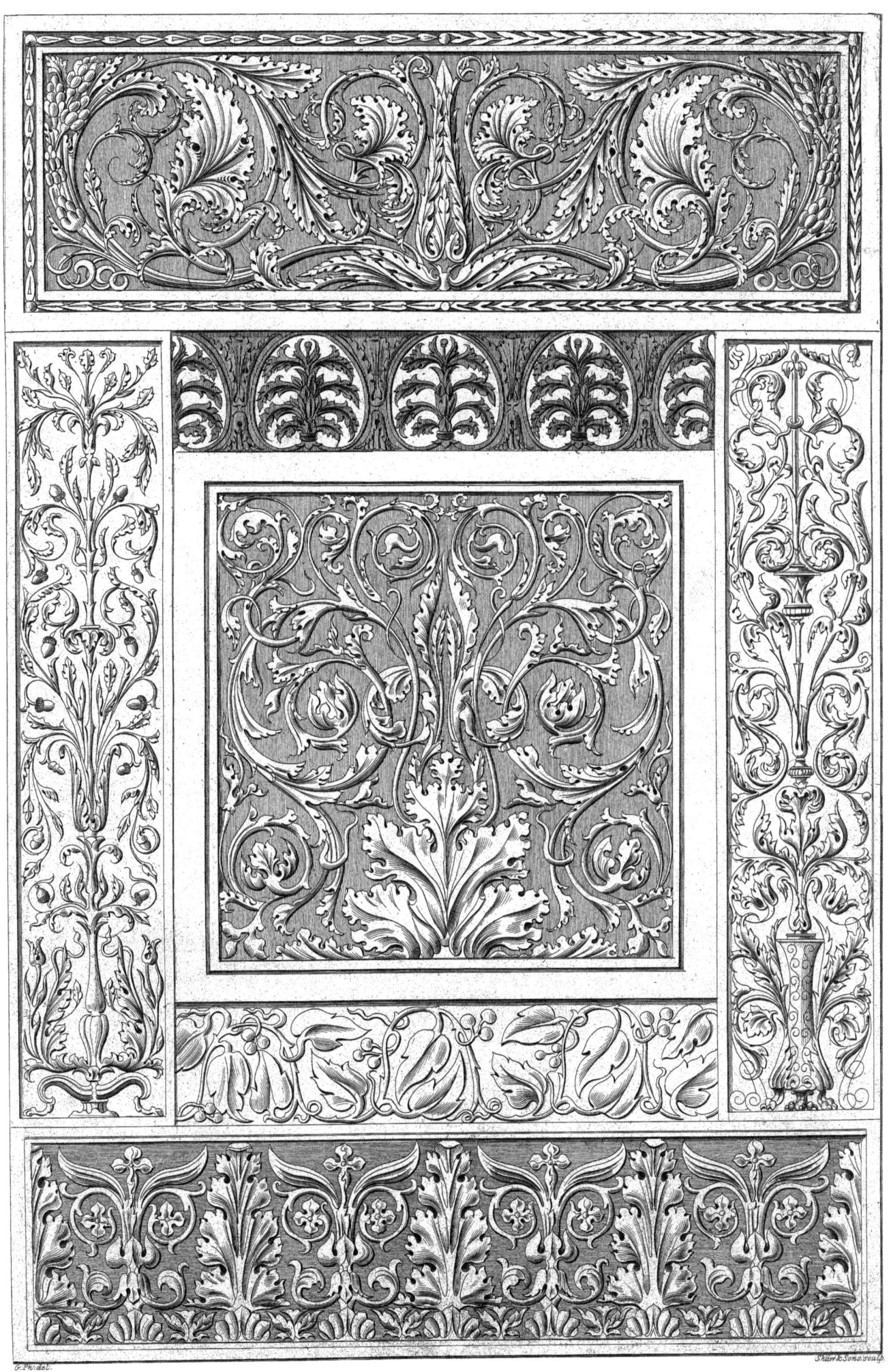

ROMAN ARABESQUE

PLATE 34

BAROQUE IN THE FLEMISH MANNER

PLATE 35

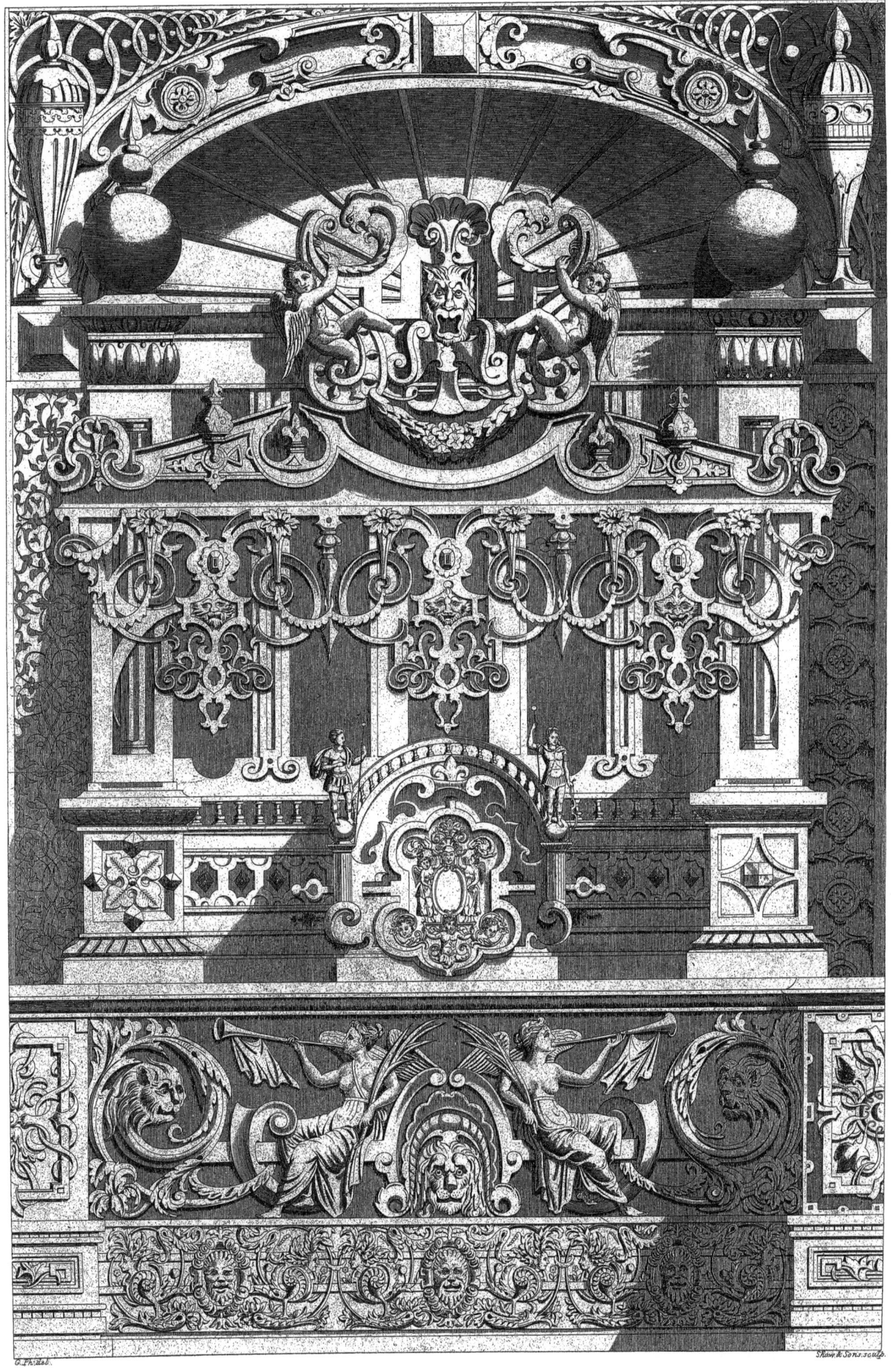

ELIZABETHAN

PLATE 36

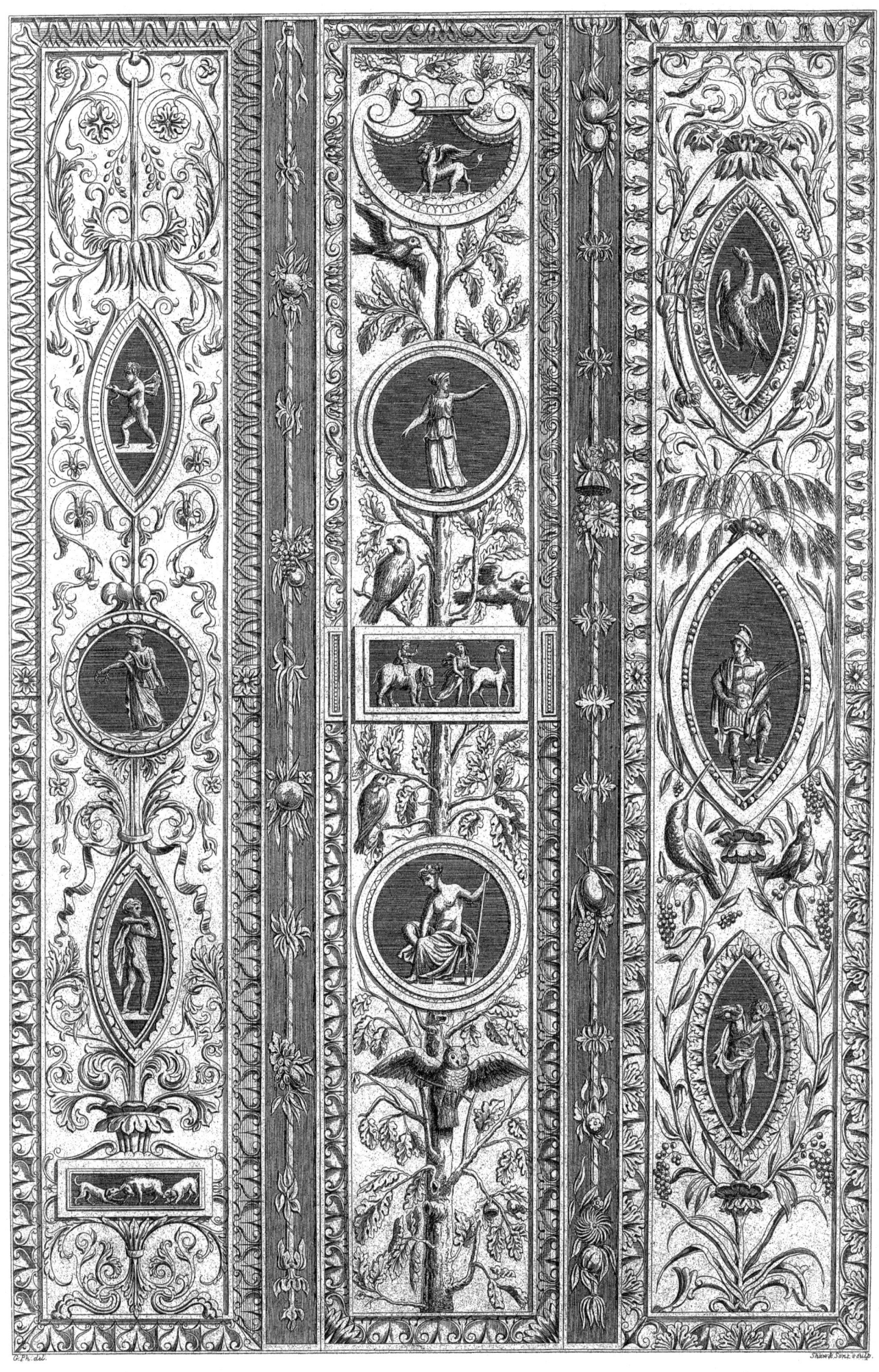

ARABESQUE IN THE MANNER OF RAPHAEL

PLATE 37

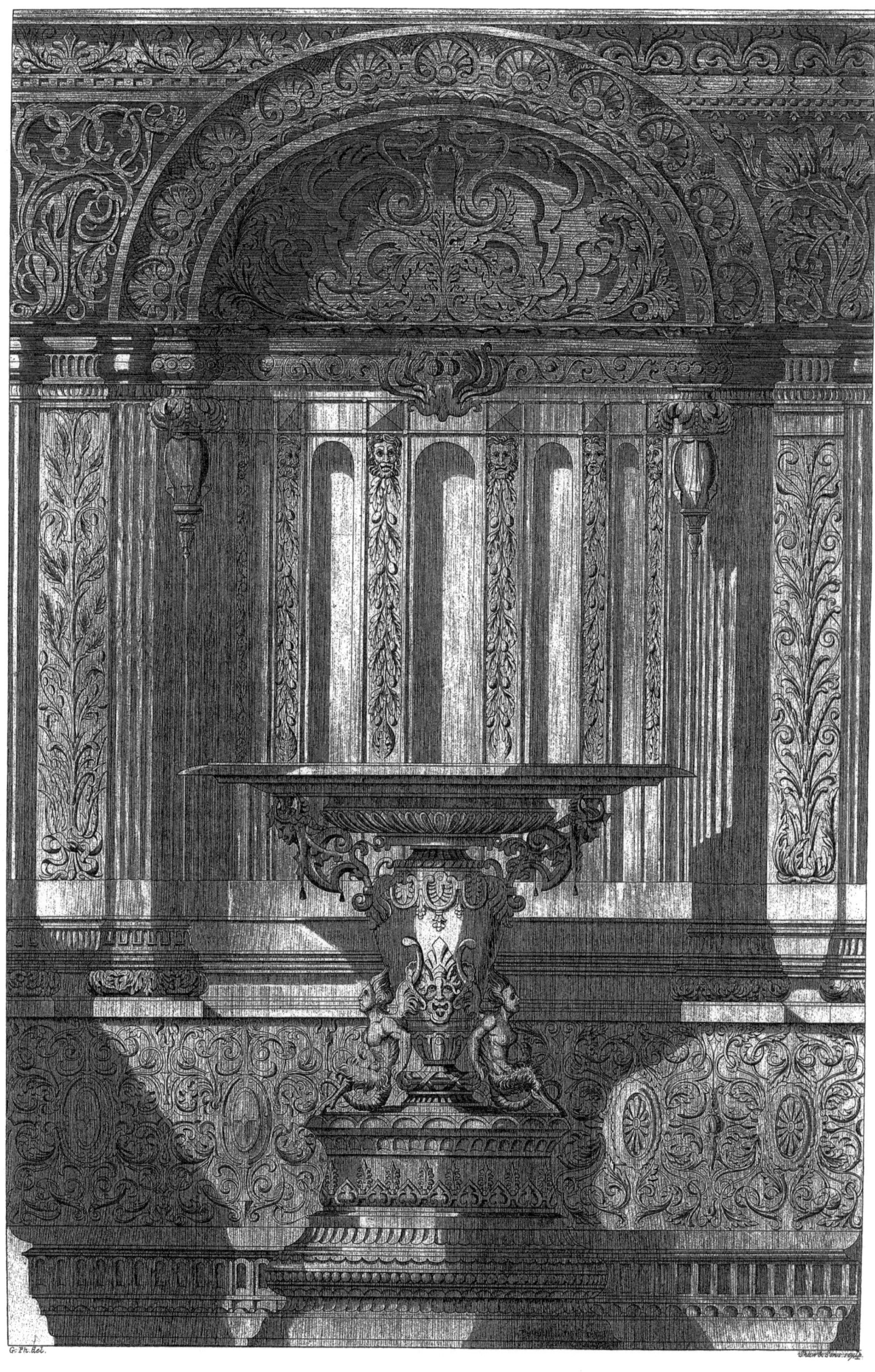

BATAVIAN

PLATE 38

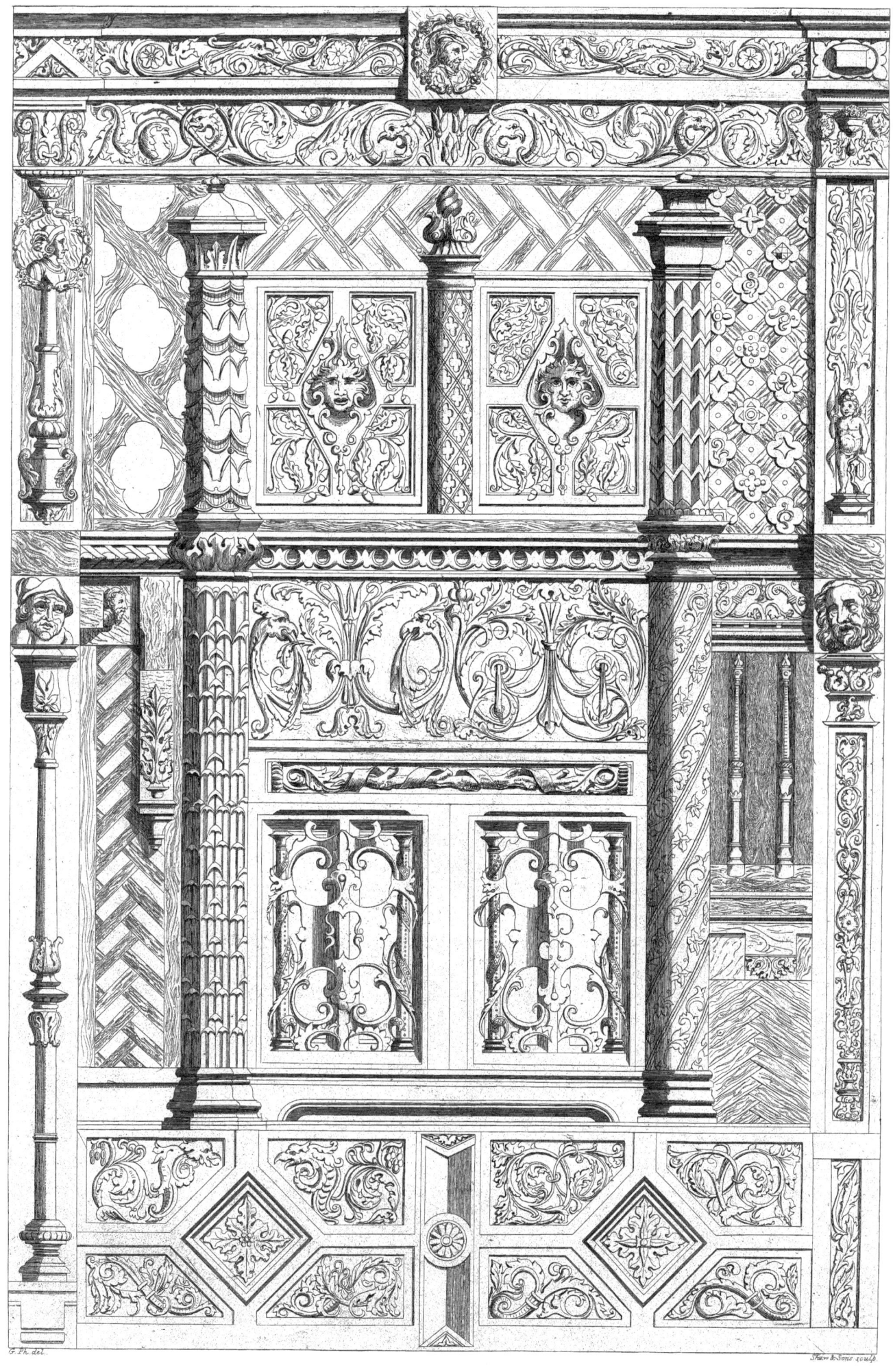

FRANÇOIS PREMIER

PLATE 39

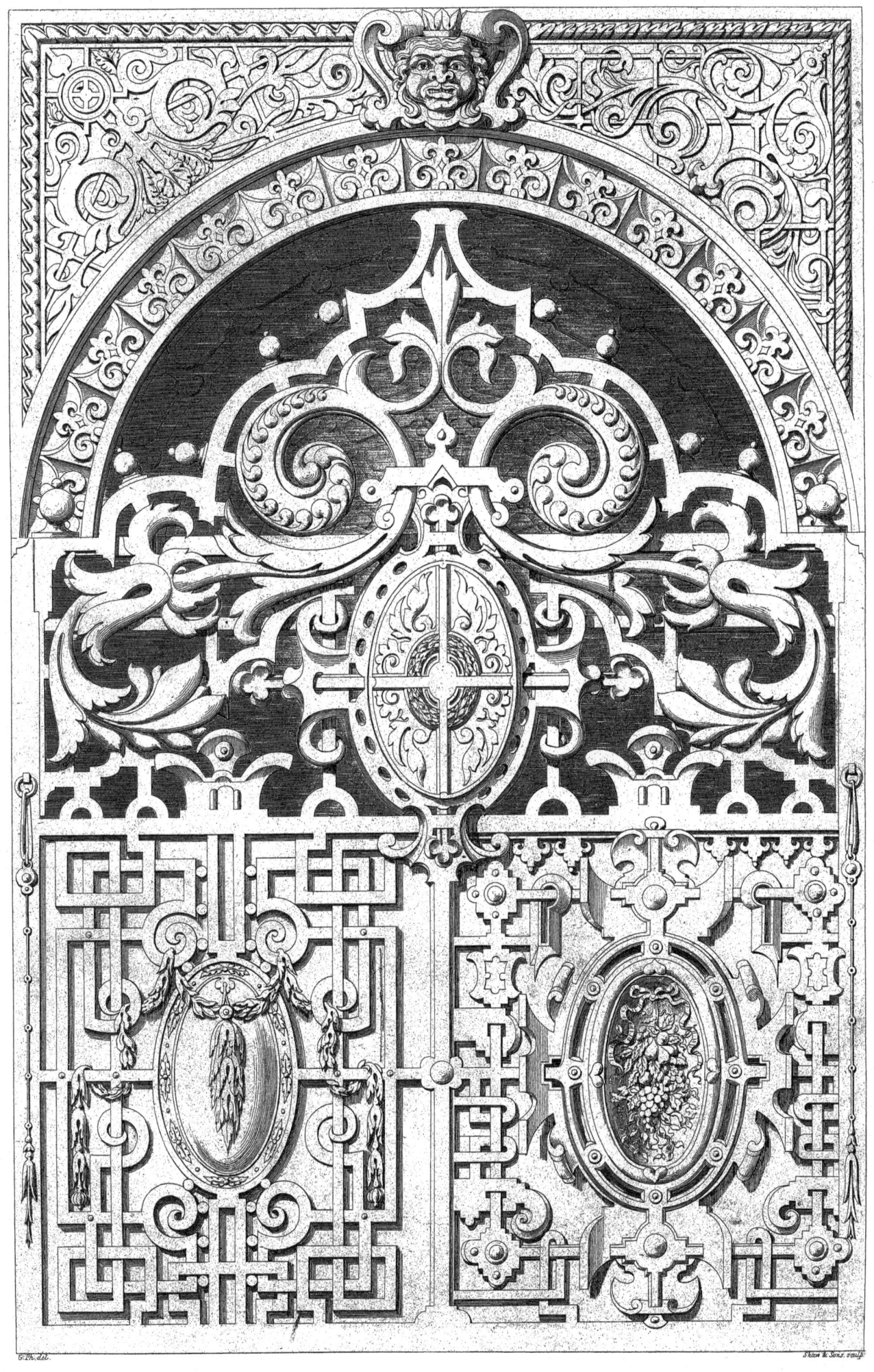

ELIZABETHAN OF VARIOUS DATES

PLATE 40

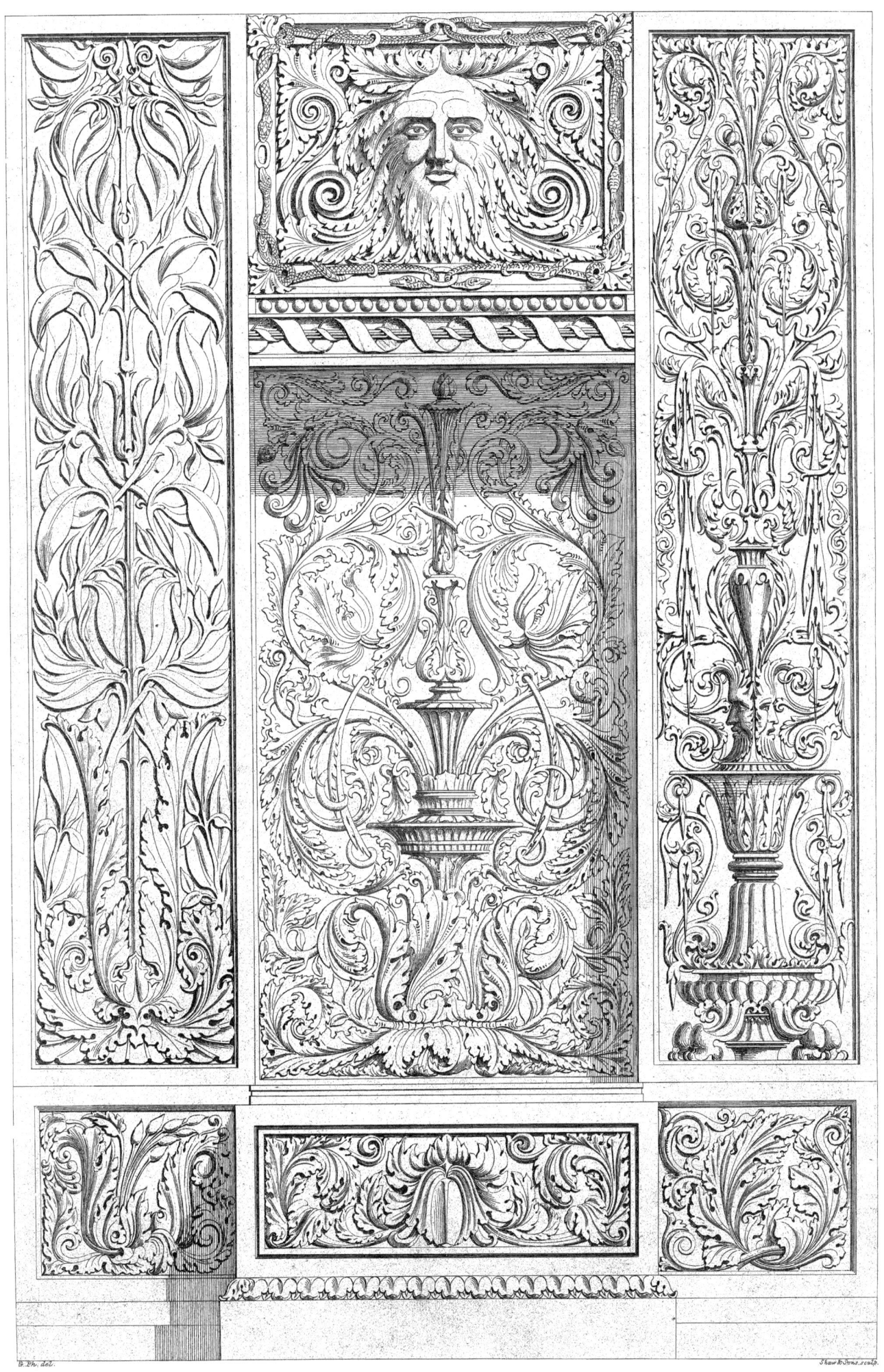

ARABESQUE IN THE ROMAN MANNER

PLATE 41

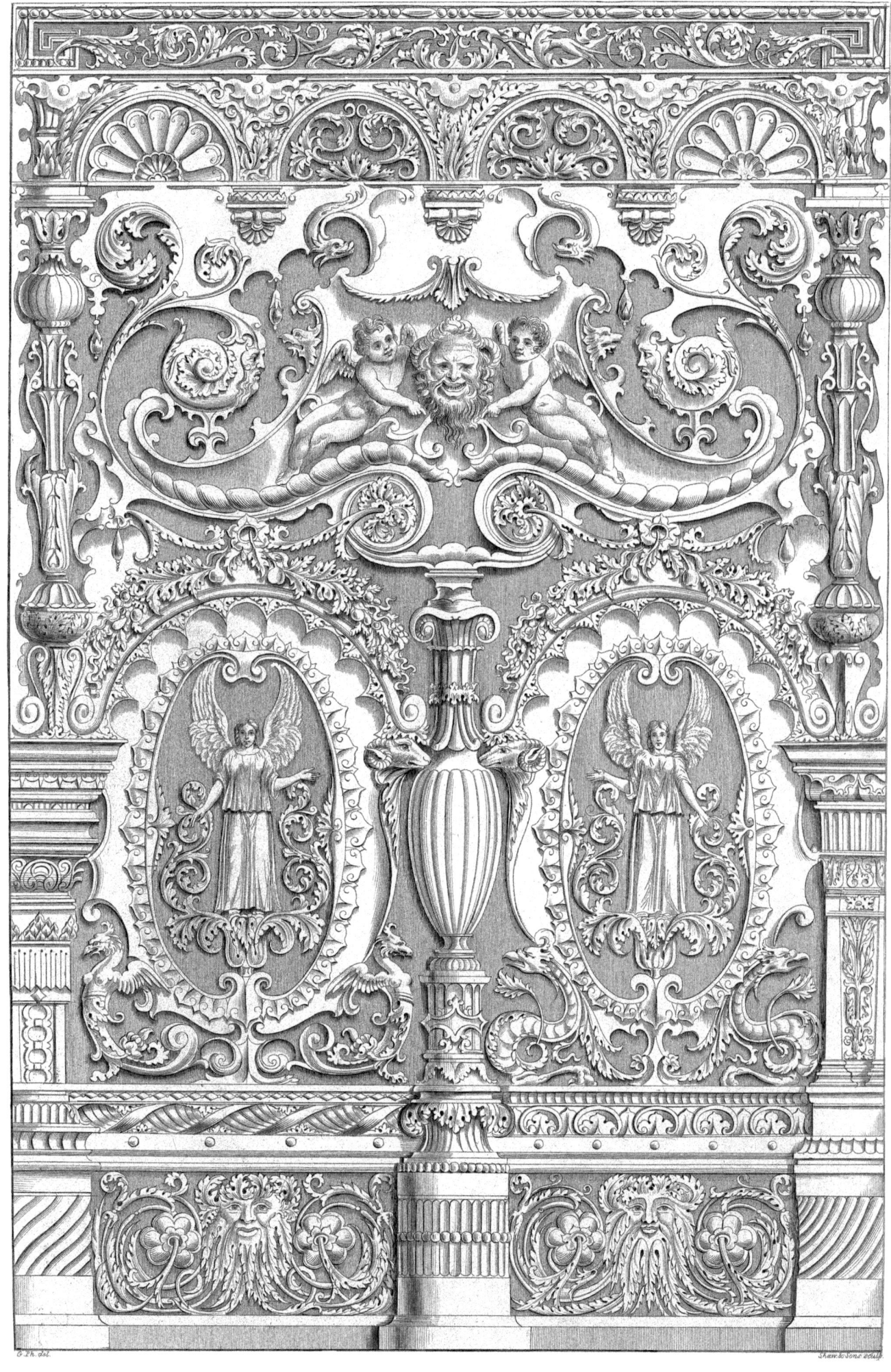

CINQUE CENTO

PLATE 42

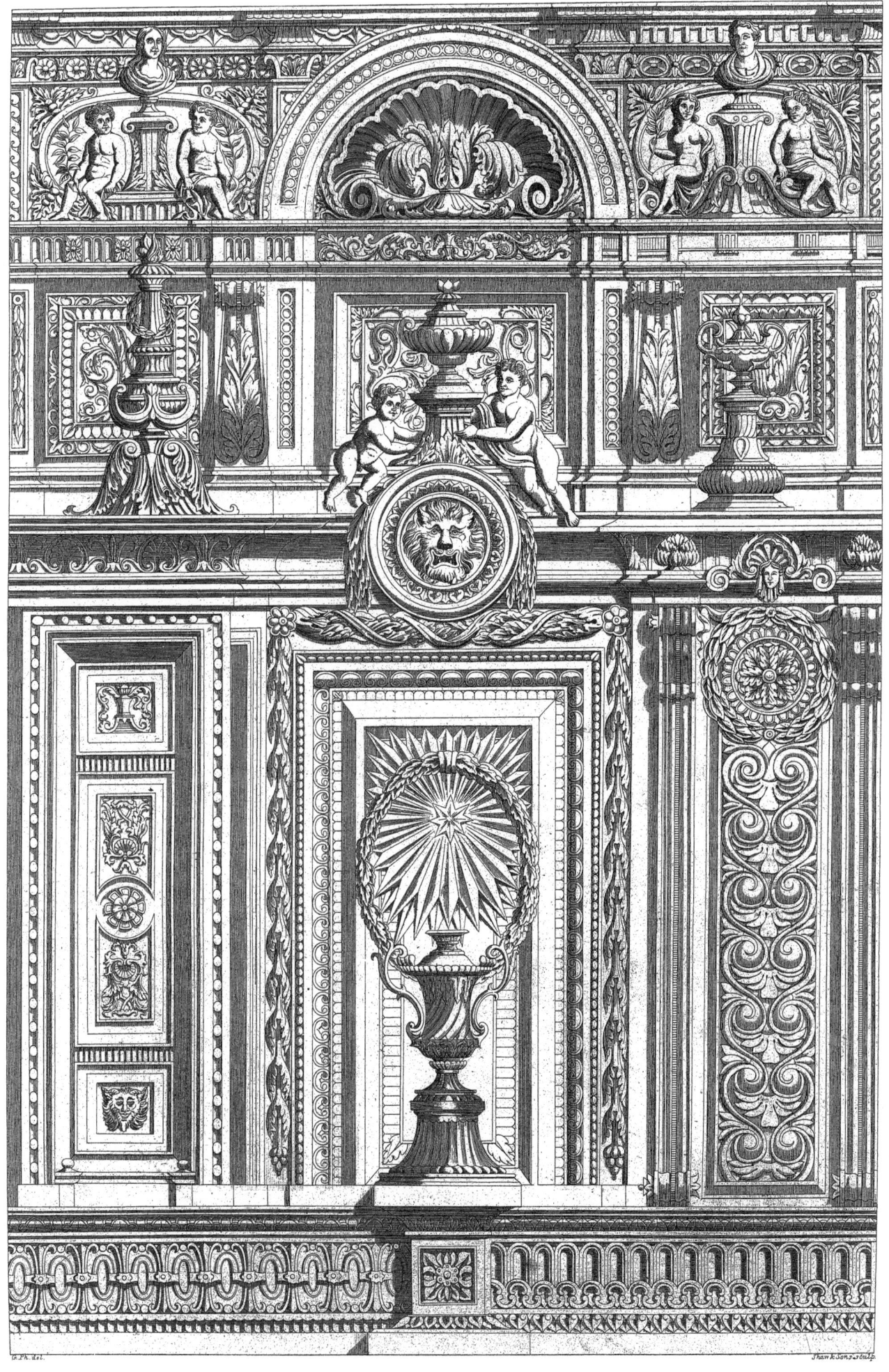

LOUIS QUATORZE

PLATE 43

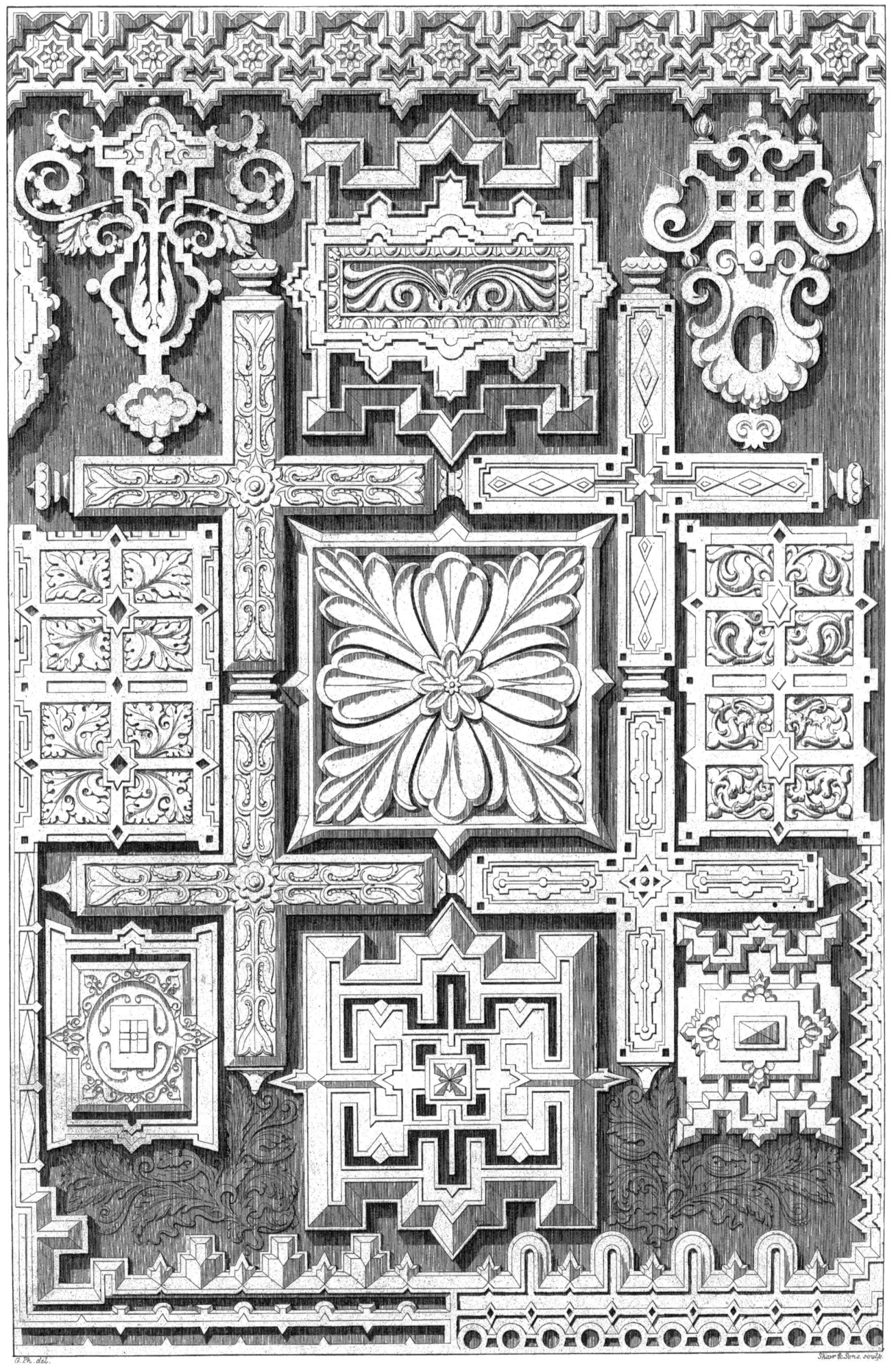

GERMAN TIMBER GOTHIC

PLATE 44

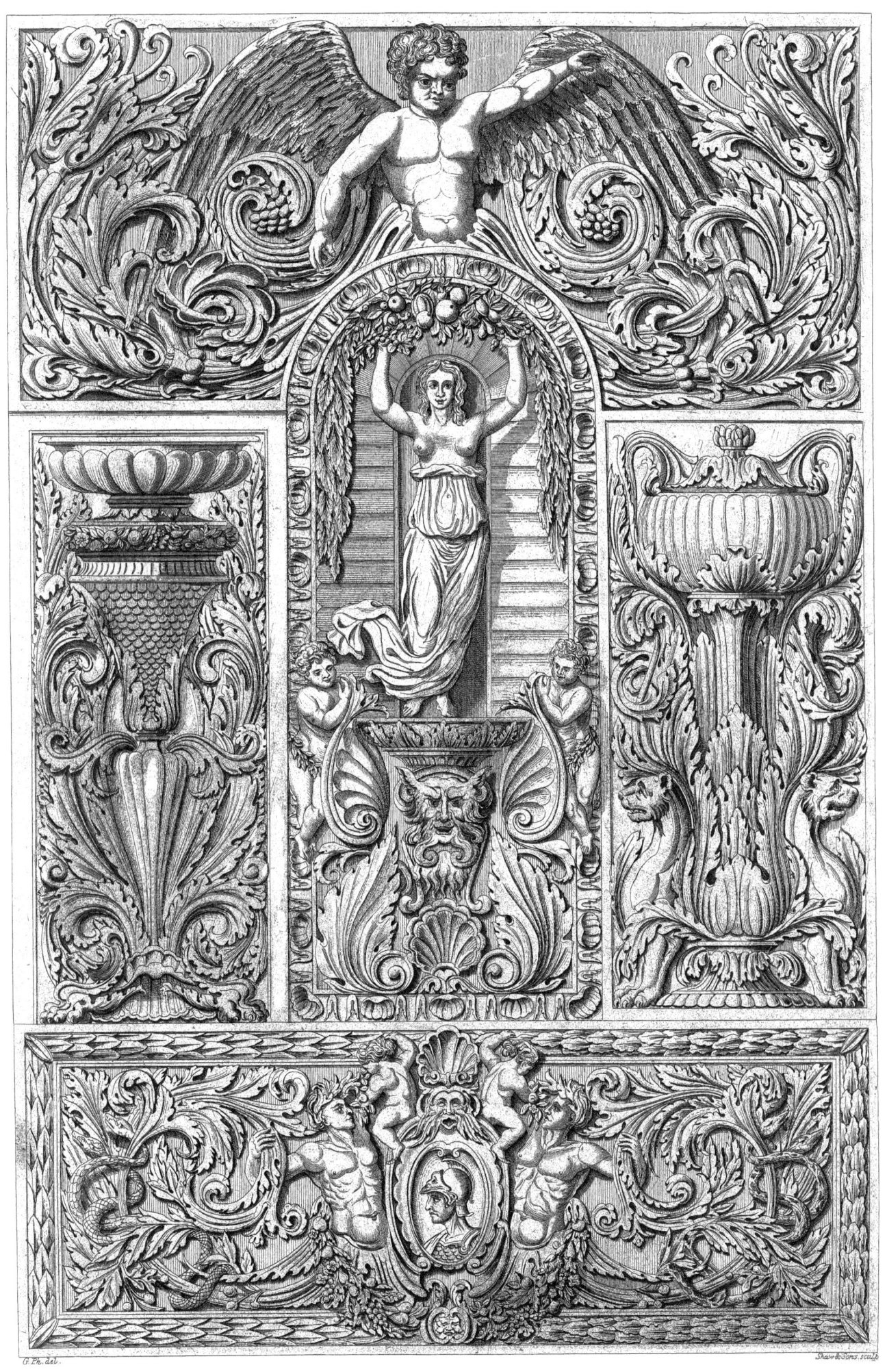

LOUIS QUATORZE IN THE MANNER OF LE PAUTRE

PLATE 45

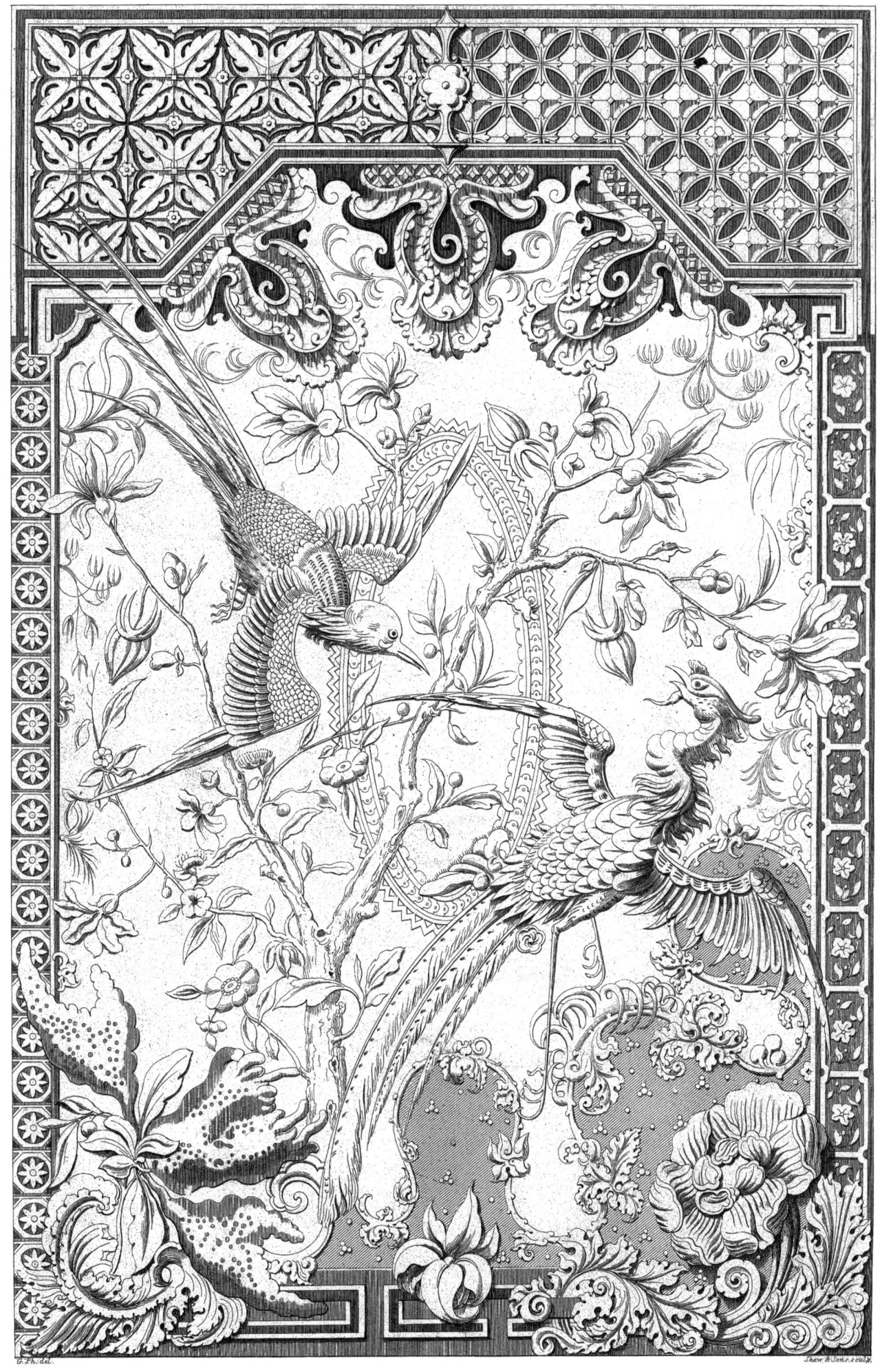

JAPANESE

PLATE 46

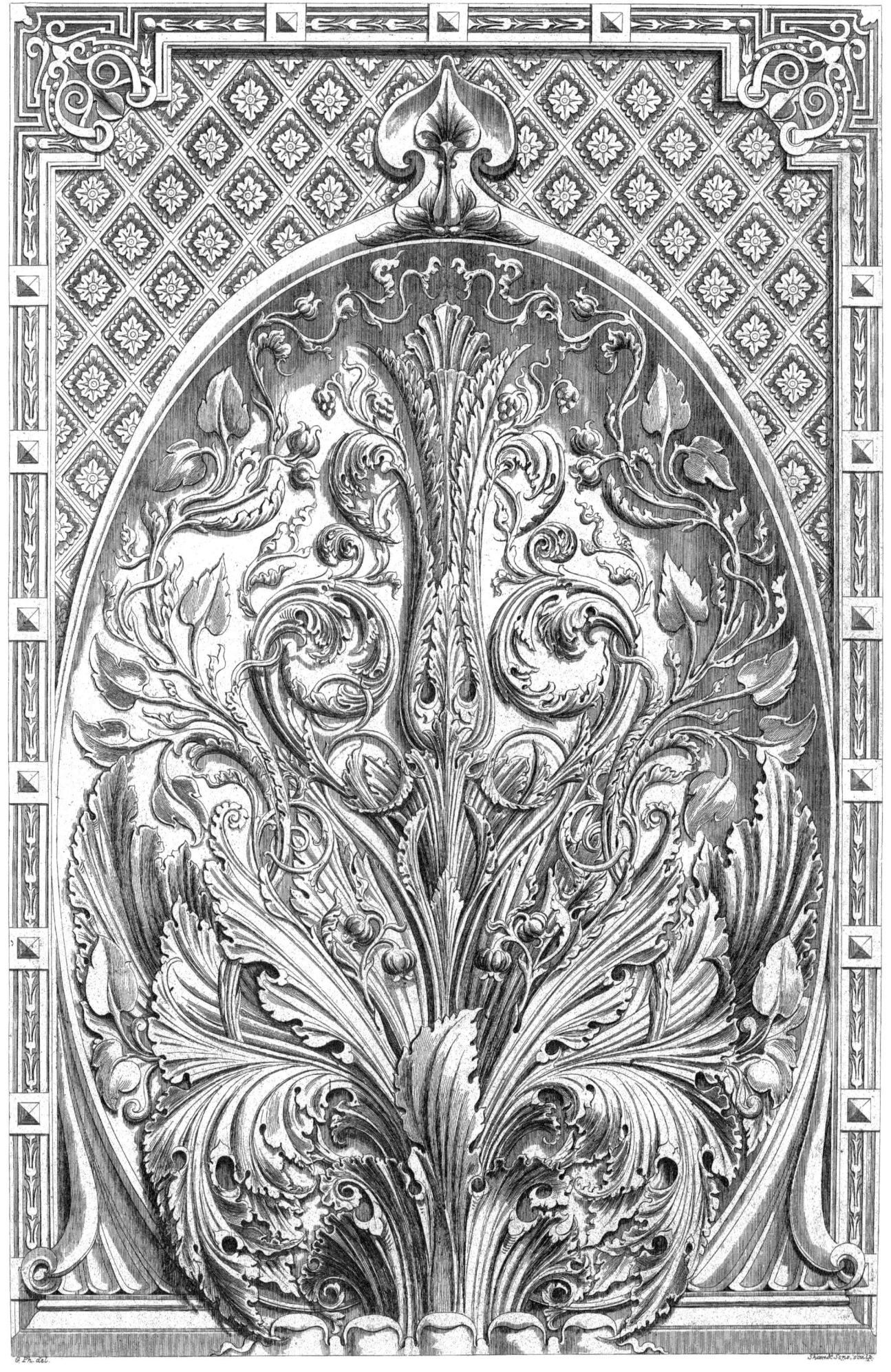

HINTS FOR A COMPOSITION

PLATE 47